Maximizing

CSS

I0488788

Profitability

Published by: Beantown Publishing LLC

http://www.beantownpublishing.com

Contents

iv

Introduction

Before we delve into the detailed writing, I'd like to make an opening comment. Unlike many other business books that have been written about high level strategies, this book is not *pie in the sky* downward look at business from 10,000 feet. Instead, this is a tactical business book that provides useful insight on **how to** efficiently and cost effectively manage a particular aspect of a business, *Customer Service and Support*. Much of what I will be sharing is based on real-life experience and observations, from the ground floor up. Ultimately, my hope is that you gain some valuable insight from my experiences, and potentially leverage some of the shared insight managing your own services business.

Over the past several decades, Customer Service & Support (CSS) has evolved from being essentially a giveaway service to producing a significant portion of overall business revenue and profit. At least that's true for most technology product companies, the vantage point from which this book is primarily written. Although, I will say, delivering service and support is fundamentally the same across most product companies. The difference between a CSS organization that supports technology versus non-technology products, the former typically requires a more sophisticated organizational design and more costly support infrastructure. Nevertheless, this book will provide useful insight and best practice recommendations that can potentially be leveraged by CSS organizations across multiple industries.

I'd like to start this journey we are about to take together by making a brief comment on why I chose to organize the book in the given manner. Since this book is about maximizing profitability, one might reasonably expect to jump right into financial details. Having spent approximately one half of my professional career in Finance roles, I can safely state, financial results strictly measure how good or bad a business is doing from a dollars and cents standpoint. It's the operational aspect of business that matters most. In other words, how efficiently and effectively business gets done. That is precisely the reason the first two parts of this book are devoted to the operational aspects of CSS businesses, with Part I focused on *Managing Business Operations*, and Part II on *Managing Human Resources*. And finally, in Part III, we will do a deep dive into *Managing the Financials*, which largely tie back to the earlier business operations and human resources discussions.

Part I starts out with a discussion about a foundational service requirement, *Design for Serviceability,* something that is critically important with regard to ease of servicing product. Regrettably, this is an area that largely receives insufficient attention. The reason being, many companies either do not understand or appreciate the value and risk avoidance benefits resulting from investing a little more up front, specifically, the product design and development phases. That is, until such time they experience a costly service disaster, which either involves a major recall or significant on-site remedial effort.

In the next five chapters of Part I, we will talk about best practices organizational design and management of each major function that make up a typical CSS organization. Our primary focus will be on cost-effective process excellence. The functional areas we will discuss in detail include: call center and knowledge base management, field service and dispatch, logistics operations, repair and refurbishment centers, and typical CSS overhead functions. In the chapter that follows, we will talk about best practices client, vendor and asset management. And, in the final chapter of Part I, we will talk about business application systems that are typically utilized by CSS organizations. Those systems include Contract and Billing Management, Field Service Management, and Call

Center Management. Some companies utilize integrated Enterprise Resource Planning (ERP) business systems, while others run their business on non-integrated systems. In any event, the above-mentioned business applications are essential to run a CSS business. The only difference between the two solutions, the former (ERP) is more streamlined and integrated than the latter, which incidentally, a great many companies are moving to integrated business solutions.

In Part II, we will talk about multiple aspects of human resource management. The reason being, the lion's share of CSS business cost is related to people. We will begin with a chapter discussing human resource justification, as it applies to existing, replacement, and additional resources. That will be followed by two chapters regarding resource cost and value management. The first of those two chapters will focus on direct labor resources, and the second on indirect (or overhead) resources. In the final chapter of Part II, we will talk about the pros and cons of utilizing external vs. internal resources. We will also address the merits and challenges associated with utilizing low-cost offshore resources. And finally, we will conclude this chapter with a discussion regarding vendor accountability for the services they provide.

In Part III, we will do a deep dive into CSS financial management, starting with a discussion regarding foundational structure. Specifically, should the organization operate as a profit center or cost center? We will then talk about the importance of a few finance fundamentals, including data integrity as well as understanding and analyzing transaction source data. Since much of the writing is related to CSS supporting product business units, rather than a standalone service business, we will then talk about how to effectively negotiate warranty cost relief or revenue sharing with the product business units. Next, we will discuss the various types of billable services, including: extended warranty, post-warranty service contracts, time & material, and service contracts for co-located other vendor products. In the final chapter of Part III, we will have an extensive discussion regarding ways to optimize CSS profitability by managing revenue and cost business drivers. Essentially, this chapter ties together everything we discussed previously, with a central focus on maximizing profitability.

Part I

Managing Business Operations

Chapter 1

Design for Serviceability

In the first six chapters, we are going to talk about core business functions that typically exist in a Customer Service & Support (CSS) organization, along with corresponding best practices. Those functions are listed immediately below. How effectively and efficiently those functions are organized and operate will have a significant impact on CSS profitability.

1. Service Design Engineering

2. Customer Service, Technical Support, and Knowledge Base Support

3. Field Service and Dispatch

4. Logistics Operations

5. Repair and Refurbishment Operations

6. Typical CSS Overhead Functions

Service Design Engineering is responsible for ensuring products are designed with serviceability in mind. From a best practices standpoint, it is critically important that service design engineers are an integral part of the product design and development process.

Why Design for Serviceability is Important

Product design engineers may do a good job designing functionality (and hopefully quality) into a product, but may overlook the ease with which service can be performed on that product. Ultimately, products that are easier to service will

1

contribute positively to profitability and customer satisfaction, which the latter will naturally lead to customer loyalty. What company wouldn't want to maximize customer loyalty, which is valued like gold by most businesses?

Design for Serviceability (DFS) takes into account the following core factors, which we will discuss in more detail shortly:

1. The ease in which routine preventive and remedial service can be performed on a product.

2. The ease and speed end-users can replace defective parts on their own.

3. Designing serviceability into a product will positively impact availability by minimizing downtime.

4. Design for serviceability should only be ignored when the cost is too great to do so.

Now let's talk about those DFS core factors in more detail. Let's assume that both preventative and remedial services are performed by certified internal and external repair technicians. There are three things that matter most when it comes to service cost. First is labor cost. Second is parts cost. And third is travel cost, if the service is being performed at the customer's site. DFS will not have any impact on parts and travel cost. Meaning, parts and any applicable travel cost will be incurred regardless of serviceability considerations in the product design.

On the other hand, DFS has everything to do with how much service labor time (cost) will be expended. Think about the labor cost difference in the following two scenarios. In the first scenario, the repair technician is servicing a product that has easily removable side panels, with components neatly mounted on racks, and the electrical wires coming off of electronic components have snap on connectors. In the second scenario, the direct opposite situation exists. Meaning, there are no removable side panels, components are hard to access and, in some cases, buried behind other components, and electrical wires have to be individuals matched and connected together with wire caps, instead of clustered into snap on connectors. Which scenario do you think is going to require more repair time and result in higher service cost? When you compound the effect of the latter scenario by thousands of service incidents, there is an enormous aggregate cost difference between the first and second scenario.

Next, let's talk about the ease and time consumed by end-users handling parts replacement on their own. To be clear, we're talking about the parts the product manufacturer has identified as end-user replaceable. In this case, the service provider does not incur service labor or travel costs. And, replacement parts cost is neutral. Meaning, the same parts are used, regardless of whether they are replaced by a repair technician or the end-user. However, what does matter, is how easy (or hard) it will be for the end-user to handle the parts replacement. The more difficult it is, the more frustrated and dissatisfied the end user will be with the product company. Here again, compound that by thousands of frustrating end-user experiences, and you will undoubtedly have a challenging customer satisfaction issue on your hands.

When customers are dissatisfied, you should also expect their loyalty to be adversely impacted. From a customer relationship standpoint, there is nothing that matters more than customer satisfaction and loyalty. Therefore, one should think long and hard before challenging customers in this manner. In other words, consider carefully which parts should truly be deemed end-user replaceable. And, make absolute sure those parts can, in fact, be replaced by the customer with relative ease.

At this point, I'd like to share a personal experience in which I was a frustrated end-user handling a part replacement. A few years back, I purchased a moderately priced well-known brand treadmill for home use, which I paid $1,500. I also purchased a multi-year on-site service contract for an additional $199. Low and behold, a couple of months after the machine was installed, the electrical display panel failed. So, I called the service company that was responsible for doing repairs. After walking me through a series of diagnostic steps, the technical service representative informed me the display panel needed to be replaced. Instead of setting up an on-site service visit, which is what I expected since I purchased an on-site service contract, the technician informed me the display panel was an end-user replaceable part. He proceeded to tell me the part would be shipped to my home address along with installation instructions. My parting question to the technician, is the display panel replacement something they expected most customers would be able to successfully handle on their own? To which the technician replied. "Absolutely!"

I have always prided myself on being relatively self-sufficient handling most repairs in and around my home. So, I initially viewed the forthcoming task as a welcome challenge. However, after successfully completing the repair, I will tell you, this was not a simple matter of removing a few screws and conveniently plugging a couple wires from the display panel to the motor control switch and flywheel sensor. I know, it already sounds complicated, doesn't it? In fact, it was fairly involved, in particular, having to snake electrical wires through the relatively narrow machine frame tubing. And, there were a series of recalibration tests and adjustments that had to subsequently be made. I don't want to make this sound like a bigger deal than it actually was. But, I will tell you, the average consumer would most likely have failed at this task. The biggest risk being, pinching the electrical wires while snaking them through the narrow frame tubing. The reason I'm telling you this story, some manufactures expect the nearly impossible from customers when it comes to self-help. Even if those customers have purchased an on-site service contract. Are you surprised?

Now let's talk about how design for serviceability can positively impact product availability by minimizing downtime. Depending on the criticality of the business the client is utilizing a particular product, the amount of downtime resulting from product failure can have a significant adverse impact on the client's business. For example, consider a modern-day company that conducts much of their business on-line. When a network server goes down, company management will surely be anxious to get the network up and running again. In which case, the sooner the network server is operational, the happier management will be. Repairing a server that is designed with ease of service in mind will almost certainly be operational sooner than if the opposite condition exists.

And finally, let's talk about situations when adding DFS features into a product is simply not cost justifiable. In this case, allow me to share a relevant personal experience, in which I replaced a kitchen faucet. I recently purchased a $450 faucet from a well-known brand name company that has a reputation for building quality products. After being on my back, under the kitchen sink, for well over an hour removing the old and installing the new faucet, I was really disappointed to see that there was hardly any pressure in the hot water line. The first thing that came to mind, I must have accidentally crimped the rigid hot water copper pipe built into the unit. Following a close inspection, I concluded that was not the problem. Therefore, I called the manufacturer and explained the problem I was experiencing. The technician led me through a series of tests, and determined the problem is related to a defective control valve. So, they shipped a free replacement valve to my home address.

Long story short, the replacement valve did not solve the problem. So, I called the manufacturer again, who then decided to send me an entire new faucet. When I asked where I should return the original unit that I purchased, the technician replied "don't bother." One would think that a $450 faucet would be built with several easily replaceable components. Well, in this case, one would think wrong! The only components that were removable were the control valve and a couple of water filters. Everything else was welded together. Clearly, when the company designed this faucet, they must have decided it's a better gamble to deal with a few throwaway defective units than incur the additional cost of building a faucet that has multiple replaceable components. Assuming that was the logic, was the design decision the right choice to make? The company will only be able to answer that question once they complete an after the fact assessment of the aggregate cost of replacement units versus the additional cost that would have been incurred building a more modular faucet.

Value of Design for Serviceability

Unfortunately, the value of DFS is not well understood and appreciated by many product companies. The principal reason, in most cases, it's difficult to assess the absolute financial benefit of designing and developing products for serviceability. While that may be true, there are countless examples of costly product recalls and on-site service sweeps that have been required to repair defective product. Think about the enormous labor cost difference of servicing easily accessible product components versus those that are difficult and cumbersome to get to. I've seen product recalls and on-site service sweeps occur several times throughout my career, and I can tell you two things about them. First, they are costly exercises. Second, depending on whether or not the product is designed with serviceability in mind, the repair can be quite cumbersome and costly. So, that brings us back to the fundamental cost versus value question, which will be repeatedly referenced throughout this writing.

In my opinion, DFS should always be considered in the product design and development process. In most cases, it behooves the manufacturer and their customers to build products that are relatively easy to service and support. The only exception is when the incremental cost of building serviceability into a product is extraordinary. In those cases, it's best to do a thorough analysis beforehand to help determine which approach would be a better from a cost versus value standpoint. Incidentally, don't forget about the potential impact these decisions may have on customer satisfaction. Customers don't like having to wait for anything, including lengthy repairs that could have been minimized with better product design. Most customers are pretty savvy. Many of them intuitively know when repairs are taking longer than reasonably expected. In which case, negative customer impressions could very well have consequential impact on future business.

Product Reliability

Reliability, Availability, and Serviceability (RAS) represent a set of attributes that is oftentimes collectively considered when designing and manufacturing a product. Generally speaking, there is usually a correlation between product reliability and availability. In other words, highly reliable products are also highly available, in terms of minimal downtime. On the other hand, serviceability is an attribute that indicates how easy (or difficult) it is to maintain and repair a product. That said, a product can be easy to maintain and repair while simultaneously deemed unreliable. Meaning, the product failure rate is too high for anyone's liking, which, of course, is never a good thing.

At this point, I'd like to briefly discuss the impact product reliability and availability have on a CSS P&. When a company produces an unreliable product, it could be good or bad for service revenue and profit, depending on whether or not most customers buy a service contract with the product. In situations whereby most customers buy a service contract, there is a high probability service cost will exceed service revenue, due to high product failures. On the other hand, if most customers do not buy a service contract, product failures will be handled on a Time and Material (T&M) basis. In which case, CSS will maximize service revenue and profit, since T&M services are typically billed at list labor and parts prices. But, I can almost guarantee, customers will not be happy in those cases. If repeat business is not terribly important to the company, this short-sighted strategy could actually work. On the other hand, if repeat business is important, it will most likely be detrimental to future business.

Now let's consider the opposite scenario in which a company produces a highly reliable product. In this case, CSS will generate maximum revenue and profit from contracted services. The simple reason, repair cost will be low due to the relatively low failure rate. Furthermore, most customers will be happy when product reliability and availability are high, making the latter a best-case scenario from both the customer and CSS standpoint.

Chapter 2

Call Center and Knowledge Base Support

Customer Service and Technical Support are typically centralized functions. That is to say, they are usually in one physical location. One notable exception is when part of those functions, and in some cases in its entirety, are offshored. We will talk more about the pros and cons of offshoring in Chapter 12, titled *Internal versus External Resources*. With regard to technical support, it is often supplemented with knowledge base support, which is accessible via the internet. Giving customers access to a user-friendly knowledge base is essential for three principal reasons. First, it's a cost-effective way of providing end-users self-help technical information. Second, some end-users are simply appalled at the thought of waiting in a long call queue to speak to a technical support agent. That is especially true for individuals who have experienced marginal benefit from speaking to live agents beforehand. Third, some end-users, especially those that are technically savvy, are more comfortable navigating through a well-designed and intuitive knowledge base than talking with another human being. Yes, these individuals may be introverts by their very nature. Nevertheless, the fact remains, there are many end-users who prefer going the self-help route. That said, it behooves most product companies to complement live technical support with a knowledge base. Next, I would like to talk about the three above mentioned customer touch points in more detail, starting with the Customer Service Center.

Customer Service Center

Customer Service Centers are typically responsible for handling any and all general service and support matters, including customer escalations. In addition, they are often responsible for contracts and billing administration, handling billing and credit disputes, as well as material return authorizations, and much more. Essentially, Customer Service Centers represent the principal point of contact for an array of non-technical service and support issues.

Incidentally, although there are some people who make a lifelong career being a customer service representative, for many others, those positions represent nothing more than an entry point into a company they aspire to grow further professionally. Aside from team managers, who are typically classified as *exempt* (or salary) employees, the individual representatives are commonly classified as *non-exempt* (or hourly, non-professional) employees. Nonetheless, they are every bit as important as higher level professional employees. The simple reason, they can leave a lasting impression on customers (good or bad), potentially influencing customer willingness to do future business with the company. On the other hand, there are many professional employees that never even talk to customers, which is to say, they have relatively less influence on the company's future success.

The challenge many companies experience with customer service representatives is keeping them sufficiently motivated to continue working at desirable performance levels. From my experience, there are a couple of highly effective motivational tools that work remarkably well in Customer Service Centers. First, monitor each individual's performance and publicly recognize the best performers each month. You can do that either via monthly group gatherings and/or publicly displaying individual achievements on centrally posted charts and graphs. These achievement charts and graphs can reflect such things as individual call volume, customer satisfaction ratings, etc. The chosen measurement elements should reflect the criteria that management deems most important.

Regardless of which method is used, these public recognitions generally achieve two results. First and foremost, they recognize and reward deserving employees for outstanding performance. Second, they motivate other aspiring employees to be among the individuals that are recognized in future months. Ultimately, whether individuals are motivated by the peer recognition and/or the financial rewards that usually accompany the recognitions, the benefits of having these programs in place usually far outweigh their cost. Bottom line, friendly competition can be fun and rewarding for the individuals involved, as well as beneficial for the company from both a financial performance and customer satisfaction standpoint.

The other highly effective motivational tool is empowerment. The average person, no matter what her role, will almost always welcome empowerment. In other words, being given a reasonable amount of authority and latitude to make business decisions on their own, instead of having to get manager approval for virtually everything they do (routine or otherwise). Managers should not be afraid to empower their employees. Done with well thought out parameters and guidelines, empowerment can be a very effective motivational tool in most organizations.

Sure, some mistakes will be made. But, better to deal with a few mistakes than having the people that work in those organizations feel like untrusted and powerless robots. The fact of the matter, checks and balances, along with corresponding reporting systems, can easily be put in place, allowing managers to monitor employee performance. If individual performance does not meet company standards, countermeasures such one-on-one post-mortem review meetings and/or additional training can be leveraged to avoid similar problems from reoccurring. On the other hand, centralized decision making will always result in more cumbersome business processes, and will certainly not be welcomed by most employees who prefer having a reasonable amount of decision making latitude.

At this point, I'd like to share a related empowerment success story. Earlier in my professional career, I was responsible for managing a combined Customer Service (CS) and Technical Support (TS) Center. The center consisted of approximately 100 agents, which included roughly 25 CS agents and 75 TS agents. The TS agents were broken down into three subgroups. One for each product line we supported, including printers, monitors, and CD-ROMs. There were two noticeable business issues that were occurring at that time. First, several of the CS Agents were in those positions for two or more years. Therefore, they were anxious to move on to something different (preferably better) to help advance their career. Second, several of the calls that were coming into the CS call queue ended up being forwarded to TS because they were technical in nature.

We did not know for certain why those technical calls were funneling through the CS call queue. We suspected it was likely due to one of two reasons. It could have been because the TS queues were typically longer. In which case, some callers decided to use the CS queue as a *back door*, knowing full well that would lead them directly to TS without having to wait in the long TS queue. Or, it could have simply been because our call routing recordings were not sufficiently clear. Nonetheless, when those particular customers reached CS, they would be required to provide a brief description of the problem they were experiencing. The call would then be forwarded to TS. Whereby, once again, the customer would have to explain their problem to the TS agent. Recognizing the straightforward nature of many of those technical calls, a couple of motivated and astute CS agents approached management with a following suggestion. Allow CS agents to directly handle straightforward technical calls instead of forwarding them to TS.

Ultimately, the suggestion was accepted, and the following adjustment was made to the organizational structure. We combined approximately ½ of the CS agents with the 1st level TS agents, and dubbed the program *One Call Solution*. We were convinced this change would benefit all parties involved, including affected employees, customers, and the company. For CS agents, it meant being empowered to handle more challenging calls, complemented with required technical training. For 1st level TS agents, it meant getting some relief handling recurring and mundane technical calls, which allowed a few of the more knowledgeable agents to advance to level 2. For customers, it meant a more streamlined and efficient call experience. And, for the company, it represented a more cost-effective process that contributed favorably to the bottom line.

We kicked off the program with free *One Call Solution* T-shirts for the entire 100 agent community. The idea being, we wanted everyone to support the change, regardless of whether or not they were directly impacted. After working through a few initial rollout kinks, the program turned out to be a resounding success. Incidentally, I am not suggesting a haphazard approach to empowerment. Obviously, it needs to be done with care, thoughtful planning, and a reasonable amount of control. However, I can safely say, done right, empowerment definitely works. And, above all, it will be welcomed and appreciated by the majority of impacted employees.

With regard to organizational structure, I have seen both efficient and inefficiently structured Customer Service Centers. Generally, the level of efficiency is influenced by three predominant factors. First, having an organizational structure that is built around meeting customer needs. Second, having internal processes and workflows that seamlessly integrate with other organizations that work closely with Customer Service such as: Technical Support, Field Operations, Business Operations, etc. Third, continuously train employees to enhance the overall knowledge and skills of the team. I cannot stress enough the necessity and benefit of continuous training. You cannot just invest in a few hours or a few days in initial training, give your CS representatives a headset, and expect them to do a good job supporting customers. There is one thing that can safely be said about most businesses, especially dynamic businesses that routinely deal with evolving products and technology, nothing remains the same for too long. Therefore, as business products, services, and processes change, so too must CS agent training keep pace with those changes.

Technical Support Center

Now let's talk about Technical Support Centers. These centers are usually broken down by product line. Let's assume your company sells personal computers, printers, and electronic storage devices. The TS organization would likely be broken down into three groups, each handling one of those product lines. Although this is a common set-up for a moderate to large technical support team, it may not make sense to do the same for a small team. The reasons being, optimal TS organizational design usually comes down to economies of scale and the all-important question, which design will produce the lowest cost per call? More on this later when we get into the details.

Companies that are required to provide 24/7 support will often adopt a so-called *Follow the Sun* strategy. Meaning, offshore resources that are located ½ way around the world are used for afterhours support. In which case, a TS organization that is proving USA based customers 24/7 support would likely staff daytime support (assume 12 hours) with USA agents, and nighttime support (the remaining 12 hours) with, let's assume, India based agents. The beauty of a *Follow the Sun* model, it's essentially always daytime in the location technical support is being provided. Furthermore, having offshore resources handle afterhours support is considerably less expensive than providing 24/7 support entirely from within the USA.

And now, let's consider a few structural options for a single shift TS organization. Once again, let's assume the company produces three product lines. In which case, TS will likely be organized in one of three ways. The first option would be having three separate groups, one for each product line. The second option would be having a single group that handles all three product lines. The third option would be having a hybrid solution, made up principally of single product knowledge technicians, and secondarily of multiple product knowledge technicians. An example of the latter for a 75 member team might be having 60 product specific technicians (20 for each of the three product lines) and 15 multiple product technicians. This hybrid solution would provide a great deal flexibility handling call volume spikes that may occur in any of the three product lines.

Given the three organizational structure options just mentioned, let's consider how each would work in two

15

different situations. One, a company that requires a total of 12 TS agents. And the other, a company that requires 75 agents. The size of the group will certainly influence what will be the optimal structure choice. In the smaller group of 12 having, more or less, 4 agents support each of the three product lines is hardly ideal in most situations. The reason being, higher than average call volume in any one of the three product lines will result in undesirably long call waiting queue for that product line. On the other hand, the product lines that are experiencing lower call volume will have agents sitting idle. Fluctuating call volume can present similar challenges for large TS teams. However, large support teams can be organized in a more fluid fashion, making them better capable of handling fluctuating call volumes.

Here is how cost and economies of scale come into play. The resource training and development cost required for the second option (a single team) would be a great deal higher than the first option (three teams). The simple reason, each member of the single team would have to possess multiple product knowledge. Furthermore, it stands to reason, individuals that possess technical knowledge for three product lines would typically command a higher salary than individuals who possess single product line knowledge. Next, I'd like to walk you through a couple of examples to crystallize this point. I'm going to run through some numbers in the next few paragraphs, so please stay with me.

Let's assume a typical agent handles 30 calls/day. Let's assume further, the average gross salary for a three product knowledge agent is $75K/year and $60K/year for a single product knowledge agent. And finally, let's assume there are 250 workdays in the year. In order to minimize complications, we're going to disregard fringe and other employee related overhead costs in these examples. Taking all of those factors into consideration, the cost for calls handled by the higher salary agents is $10/call ($75,000/250/30), while the cost for calls handled by the lower salary agents is $8/call ($60,000/250/30). Given no additional information, this simple calculation would obviously have you conclude that option one (three teams) would be the more cost-effective structure. Maybe so, but before we immediately jump to that conclusion, let's consider a couple other factors that typically come into play in real world situations.

One factor is the agents' productive versus idle time, and the other is the amount of time customers have to wait in the call queue. Incidentally, it goes without saying, the longer the call queue wait time, the more irritated customers become. At any rate, it's not unusual for a multi-product company to have quality and performance issues with a given product line, while the other product lines are free and clear of such issues. That means one team will be overwhelmed with calls and long wait queues, while the other teams experience an unusual amount of idle time. So, the question becomes, what is the average cost/call in this scenario?

Given the above stated assumptions, the cost/call for the overwhelmed team is unchanged at $8/call. Meaning, the team is achieving maximum call volume, while the call waiting queue grows increasingly longer. On the other hand, let's say the other two support teams are experiencing 20% idle time. In that case, the average cost/call for those two teams goes from $8 to $10/call. Here is how the math works ($60,000/250/30/.8). So, when you recalculate the overall average cost for the three combined teams, it's $9.33/call ($8 + $10 + $10)/3. Therefore, the previous calculated $2/call cost advantage of having three product teams versus a single team has shrunk down to $.66 ($10.00 - $9.33). All of a sudden, what once appeared to be a cost compelling advantage, has essentially been neutralized. And, considering the inevitable dissatisfaction experienced by customers who are having to wait in the long call queue, the three team approach would likely not be considered to be the optimal solution.

Considering the potential adverse cost and/or customer satisfaction impact of going with options on either end of the spectrum (meaning one or three teams), a middle of the road hybrid solution may be best. For demonstration purposes, let's examine how a hybrid solution would impact a TS team that has a total of 75 agents. Here again, we're going to assume the agents are supporting three product lines. In which case, a reasonable hybrid solution might look something like the following. Twenty agents with single product knowledge are assigned to each of the three product line sub-teams, and the 15 agents with multiple product knowledge are utilized wherever the need is greatest. That way, you have the potential of almost instantly doubling the support agents to handle a particularly challenging or troubled product line. If there are no unusual product issues, those 15 multi-product agents can be equally distributed across the three product line sub-teams.

Bottom line, from a process standpoint, this hybrid solution provides a great deal of flexibility, while minimizing the potentially negative customer satisfaction impact resulting from long call waiting queues. Once again, let's do the math for the hybrid solution. I'm going to assume call waiting and idle time challenges are essentially neutralized with this hybrid support structure. Using the same cost/call assumptions that were calculated above, namely, $8/call for single product knowledge agents and $10/call for multi-product knowledge agents, the average cost/call for this hybrid solution would be approximately $8.50 ($8 + $8 + $8 + $10)/4. That would make the hybrid model the best overall solution, resulting in a reasonably low cost/call, and providing maximum call handling distribution capability. Incidentally, considering each company has unique challenges and circumstances, the ideal solution for a given company may not be this black and white. Nevertheless, a middle of the road hybrid solution will almost always work better than a rigid non-flexible solution.

At this point, I'd like to talk about tiered technical support, which is very common in large service organizations, regardless of whether they are supporting hardware and/or software products. Generally, there are three tiers (or levels) of technical support: L1, L2, and L3. L1 typically consists of generalists who handle the more common and less complicated technical problems. The people on L1 teams normally possess a moderate level of technical knowledge and rely heavily on knowledge base and resolution scripts. From a cost standpoint, a service provider would want their L1 team to handle the maximum number of technical calls. The reason being, cost/call is generally considerably lower than when an L2, and in particular a L3 technician gets involved in a call. In terms of resource distribution, I would say roughly 75% of the total number of technicians are typically on the L1 team.

The L2 team is generally considerably smaller, and consists of individuals who are more highly skilled and more highly compensated than L1 agents. For example, if the average salary for L1 agents is $50K/year, L2 agents are likely paid an average salary of, more or less, $75K/year. The people on L2 teams normally possess expert level product support knowledge. Furthermore, they often have a good understanding of how the company's products integrate with other vendor hardware and/or software products, which can be especially helpful resolving complicated integration issues and challenges. Unless there are contractual arrangements with specific clients to do otherwise, calls typically start with L1 agents. In cases the L1 agent cannot resolve the problem, the call is handed off to an L2 agent for deeper level troubleshooting and resolution. And, in rare cases the L2 agent cannot resolve the problem, the call is handed off to an L3 agent who possesses the deepest level product support knowledge, and is oftentimes a member of the hardware or software development team.

What I just described is a typical organizational design for large companies whose products are technical and/or relatively complicated. In other cases, there is either only one or two levels of technical support. Depending on the products and type of clients being supported, these teams can be set up any number of ways. In some contractual arrangements, the client will staff a Help Desk that will front-end and attempt to resolve as many problems as possible. In those cases, the call moves to the service provider's technical support team only if the client's Help Desk cannot resolve the problem. In other contractual arrangements, the reverse is true. In other words, the service provider is responsible for the front-end Help Desk support, while the client is staffed to only handle the more complicated issues. There is no one right or wrong way to set up these support teams. Any/all variations work under the right circumstances.

No matter what the organizational design, besides hiring the best possible resources, the two biggest challenges Technical Support organizations typically face is maintaining a high level of productivity and employee motivation. And yes, the two are intrinsically connected to one another. From my point of view, which is derived from extensive experience managing support centers, the most effective way to positively affect both challenges are with reward and recognition programs. In most cases, a pat on the back for work well done is simply not enough, even if it's delivered publicly amongst peers. The fact of the matter, accompanying rewards with recognition is much more effective. In most cases, we're not talking about large sums of money. Relatively modest monetary rewards in the $100 - $500 range, or tickets to a major league sporting event, work wonders to both motive people and instill a sense of friendly competition amongst the team members. Ultimately, the best run and most effective organizations strive to accomplish two things, performance excellence and having each individual be the best they can be. Without a doubt, reward and recognition programs help toward that end, and in most cases are cost justifiable.

In good conscience, I cannot leave this subject without mentioning some of the negative aspects of technical support that frustrate many customers. In this regard, I suspect each reader has his own pet peeves. For me, and probably many of you, those pet peeves include the following: long hold times, repeat calls, and dealing with inept and cavalier support technicians. I am quite confident these three issues are among the most frustrating for many customers. Therefore, we will discuss each of them in more detail. And, I will provide what I believe to be pragmatic solutions for each of these rather annoying issues.

Let's start with long hold times. There are two aspects of long hold times that frustrate customers. First and foremost, sitting idle waiting for a technician to speak with about a problem or issue the customer is experiencing. Second, using up precious minutes on the customer's telephone service plan. Incidentally, regarding the latter, if you're using your cell phone, which many people do nowadays, toll-free 800 numbers are not free calls. Those minutes are charged to your cell plan, just as toll call minutes are. Also, I don't know about you, but the constant interruptions by automated recordings telling you, over and over again, that you are a valued customer, and suggesting you go to their web site for self-help instead of waiting in the call queue really adds to the frustration.

First of all, the nonsensical statement about being a valued customer is nothing more than an empty and meaningless gesture, which most people find offensive because they know better. Regarding web self-help suggestions, isn't it obvious that most people would have gone to the web beforehand, assuming they are comfortable doing so? To be completely fair, in some cases, the little pointers you receive while you're waiting on the call can be useful. However, that's more so the exception than the rule. For the most part, those pointers represent valueless information.

Instead of simply beefing up staff and increasing support cost, there are a few other viable ways of addressing long hold times. The first, and highly effective option, is instituting an automated customer callback process. If you're not familiar with this process, it gives customers the option of getting a callback instead of waiting on hold. The beauty of this process, the customer does not lose her position in the call queue and she receives an estimated callback time. For those customers, this process represents a precious time saver, as well as prevent unnecessary consumption of phone plan minutes. For vendors who offer toll-free 800 service, which most do, it saves a great deal of telephone expense, which would otherwise be incurred having people waiting in the call queue.

Let's consider a dollarized example. Assume the service provider pays $.05/minute for the 800 line. Assume further, they receive 2,000 calls/day with an average wait time of 15 minutes. That represents 30,000 unproductive minutes per day at a cost of $1,500/day. Assuming 250 workdays/year, that's $375,000/year, which is money that could have otherwise been spent on a more cost-effective automated callback system, not to mention the resulting improvement in customer call experience that system would provide.

Another effective way of addressing long hold times is to routinely review your daily call distribution and adjust staffing according to historical spikes. For your particular business, those spikes could be certain hours of the workday or certain days in the workweek. Regardless, it's a good bet that adjusting staffing to more or less mimic historical call distribution will likely contribute to lower call hold times, which will save you money on 800 number phone expense, as well as improve the overall customer call experience.

Now, let's move on to repeat calls. Most customers who have dealt with repeat calls for the same problem will tell you their experience was frustrating. Generally speaking, it's absolutely reasonable for a customer to expect a problem or issue to be resolved with a single call into Technical Support. Unfortunately, too often, that is not the case. By the time you get to the second agent, you're already wondering if the technicians you're speaking with know what they are doing. And, if you've had the unenviable experience of talking with a third or a fourth agent regarding the same problem or issue, you're likely well beyond frustrated.

Although repeat calls are commonplace in many support organizations, for the most part, they are totally unnecessary and are the result of ill-prepared and/or ill-trained support organizations, which the fault rests squarely on management's shoulders. Sure, there are unusually complicated situations legitimately requiring a second and possibly third call before the matter is finally resolved. However, that's more so the exception than the rule. From my experience, I'd have to say the majority of repeat calls are due to inept or insufficiently trained technicians, which management could easily correct with additional call monitoring and technician feedback, as well as additional training.

And finally, let's talk about those annoying inept and cavalier technician. It's probably safe to say, at one time or another, we have all had the displeasure of dealing with an inept or cavalier technician. Calls with inept technicians are typically long and cumbersome, often due to lack of technical knowledge and/or experience. You generally know when you have one of these technicians on the other end of the line. They are the ones that often place you on hold to seek help or guidance from a supervisor or more knowledgeable colleague. There are a few different ways a service provider can tackle this problem. The most obvious, make sure your technicians are properly and sufficiently trained before you have them take customer calls. It's important to understand, inadequately trained support personnel will typically increase instead of decrease your support cost. The simple reason, a matter that should take five minutes to resolve can easily turn into a needlessly long, costly, and frustrating customer experience taking an hour or more to resolve. When that happens, no one wins. The service provider's cost becomes inordinately high, and the customer's call experience is undesirable, to say the least.

In addition to having properly trained support personnel, there is a right and wrong way of ensuring technicians are ready to take customer calls. The wrong way is to have them go through some basic training, hand them a headset, and have them immediately start taking customer calls. The right way is to gradually develop their skills and knowledge to the point you are confident the technicians are sufficiently trained and skilled to handle customer support calls.

A step by step process I've seen work very well goes something like what follows. The first step, have the new technician listen in on several live customer calls that are being handled by a more experienced technician. The second step, have the new technician handle live customer calls along with a more experienced agent listing in and guiding him throughout the call process. The third step, have the technician handle customer calls on his own, but make sure the calls are recorded and subsequently reviewed by the quality assurance manager or the technician's supervisor. The fourth step, provide the technician immediate feedback regarding what was done well and areas that need improvement. The final step, if and when deemed necessary, develop an individualized improvement plan for specific technicians that focus on activities they have demonstrated need improvement. Sometimes it's a matter of improving technical knowledge, while other times it's improving people skills, which both are key ingredients for a good customer support call experience.

Cavalier technicians are the ones that I personally find particularly annoying. Here again, you can usually tell when you have one of these gems on the other end of the line. They are the ones that are obviously preoccupied with something else that is going on around them, and clearly not paying attention to what you are saying. How do you know that? A good clue is being asked to repeat yourself. An even better clue, the technician attempts to play back something you said, which clearly demonstrates he was not paying attention.

Another annoying behavior is when a cavalier wise guy or gal is obviously talking down to you because you don't understand their technical jargon. In this case, you might have had to ask the technician more than once for an explanation or direction walking you through a problem resolution. In any case, that type of behavior is totally unprofessional and essentially guaranteed to reflect badly on subsequent customer service surveys. An effective way of addressing this problem is the team supervisor and/or quality manager randomly listen to recorded calls, paying close attention to the technician's courtesy and behavior. If courteous and proper behavior is lacking, be sure to quickly address and resolve those matters with the technician.

Like most bad behavior that is not immediately addressed, you can count on it getting worse before it gets better. Once you have uncovered unacceptable behavior, you have two likely courses of action. One, sit down with the technician to inform him where he went wrong, and tell him to quickly and permanently clean up his act. If that doesn't work, terminate their employment before they do more damage. Remember, from the customer's point of view, the technician's behavior is a reflection of how you run your company more so than that particular technician's behavior. That's why it is critical to move quickly and decisively to address these undesirable matters.

Knowledge Base

One of the most worthwhile investments a service organization can make is build and maintain a robust and user-friendly knowledge base, which is accessible to both their technical support agents and customers. Ideally, you would want your knowledge base to contain a partition. Meaning, only part of it is accessible to customers, while the entire knowledge base is accessible to your technical support agents. The reason for the partition, there may be proprietary information your agents need to support customers that you do not want your customers to have direct access. Regardless of how it is structured (with or without a partition), making a robust knowledge base available to your customers, particularly tech savvy clients, will almost certainly contribute to lowering your technical support call volume and overall support cost.

Incidentally, tech savvy users often prefer a knowledge base to talking with a live support agent. That may be because they believe that they possess more technical knowledge than the average agent they are likely to get on the phone. Or, they may simply be introverts who don't like talking with other people. Incidentally, my comment regarding introverted personalities is not meant to be disrespectful. Throughout my professional career, I have worked closely with many tech savvy people who I have a great deal of respect. The fact of the matter, it's not uncommon for many of those individuals to be more comfortable working alone than intermingled with others.

On the other hand, non-tech savvy customers, regardless of their personality trait, have little choice when it comes to technical support. For these individuals, attempting to navigate their way through a knowledge base, no matter how intuitive it may be, will cause them to easily become intimidated and quickly frustrated. In which case, those individuals will definitely prefer help and guidance from a live technical support agent.

All things considered, a web accessible knowledge base is a smart and worthwhile investment for most modern-day companies. That is especially true nowadays, since the majority of people regularly access the web for virtually any/all kinds of information (personal and business). The same could not have been said 20 years ago.

Chapter 3

Field Service and Dispatch

There are two fundamental principles that must be taken into account when developing a field service and dispatch strategy. The first is maximizing remote resolutions, while minimizing on-site dispatch. The second is maximizing on-site coverage at the lowest possible cost. With regard to the latter, a common component of a cost-effective on-site support strategy oftentimes includes selective utilization of third-party service providers. The principal focus of this chapter will be on the two above stated principles, as well as factors that should be taken into account when considering the use of third-party service providers. We will also briefly discuss when it makes sense for a service organization to have an escalation management function.

Maximize Remote Resolutions and Minimize Dispatches

The more service incidents can be diagnosed and resolved remotely, the lower will be the cost of service. That is why it behooves a service organization to put some of their most knowledgeable repair technicians in their Diagnostics and Dispatch Center. Even if the repair requires some hands-on customer assistance, remote resolution is the most expeditious and cost-effective way to go. Incidentally, there are two ways to incent customers to support a repair effort. The first is with financial incentives baked into the service contract. In other words, a lower price for contracts that contain a stipulation such as the following. "Whenever reasonably possible, the customer must provide assistance with on-site repair." The other way is by convincing customers, on an individual repair incident basis, that providing a little hands-on assistance will get them up and running quicker than having to wait for an on-site technician to come to their premises.

All too often, field operations organizations have a front-end diagnostics and dispatch process that does virtually nothing more than dispatch on-site field technicians, whether or not those technicians are truly required. This is a huge problem/opportunity for many service organizations. One of the principal cost management objectives of a field operations organization should be to minimize on-site dispatches. So, how can one effectively avoid on-site dispatches and still meet customer support needs? The answer is, do as much up-front diagnostics as possible before dispatch. Makes sense, right? But, here is the problem with many Diagnostics and Dispatch Centers. The depth of diagnostics that is actually done is oftentimes severely lacking. The reason being, these centers are typically staffed with relatively low-level technicians who are not sufficiently skilled or trained to provide thorough remote diagnostics and problem resolution support.

The solution to this problem is moving some of your better technicians to the Diagnostics and Dispatch Team. That way, you will be able to maximize remote resolutions, which is considerably less expensive than needlessly dispatching field technicians. I made this vary change in one of the support centers I previously managed and, will tell you, it resulted in a marked improvement. However, I must warn you, if you decide to move some of your better technicians into Diagnostics and Dispatch, you will likely encounter the following two challenges. First, there is a fundamental misconception regarding remote technicians. Specifically, those individuals are presumed to be relatively lower skilled professionals than on-site technicians. Although that is oftentimes true, it does not have to be that way. Hence, your first challenge is convincing some of your better technicians to move to Diagnostics and Dispatch. More on "how to" accomplish that in a few moments. Second, although these teams are often housed in a single physical location, the use of modern-day virtual tools and technology have made it possible for team members to work virtually, instead of a central physical location.

My advice, keep an open mind about the merits of virtual support. Also, do everything reasonably possible to entice some of your highly skilled on-site technicians to join the Diagnostics and Dispatch Team. In which case, you may have to offer those individuals relocation assistance. Even given that incentive, you may still encounter resistance from several individuals.

In the old days, when a company wanted an employee to move to a different location, there was usually little resistance because that was thought to be the faster and more direct route to career advancement. Generally speaking, that is no longer the case. Modern-day employee attitudes toward relocation have changed dramatically. Getting people to uproot away from family and friends is a much bigger deal than it used to be. Also, technological advances have made working virtual seamlessly possible for many functions never previously imagined. Bottom line, getting employees to agree to relocate nowadays will generally require some motivational incentives. You can say all you want about the merits and criticality of having talented individuals like them on the front-end (diagnostics and dispatch). But, unless you are willing to put some money on the line, sought after employees will likely not take the bait. Meaning, you probably have to offer those individuals a solid compensation package, potentially accompanied with performance incentives. In the final analysis, I can confidently state, putting some of your best talent on the front-end is almost guaranteed to improve operational efficiency and correspondingly reduce cost.

Maximize Coverage Area at Lowest Possible Cost

Now let's talk about the actual field organization. As with any geographical staffing challenge, the number one objective should be maximizing coverage at the lowest possible cost. Sounds good, right? But, how does one actually go about doing that? Ideally, you would want to correlate the number and concentration of your field technicians with the concentration of product in the installed base. In some cases, there is a sufficient amount of product in a particular client building or campus location to justify one or more dedicated field technicians. The same is true for urban areas that have a significant concentration of the company's products. Often times, urban areas will justifiably have fully staffed local district offices with several technicians.

On the other hand, it's an altogether different challenge staffing on-site support for less concentrated suburban and/or rural areas. In those situations, there is one other significant matter that comes into play, unproductive travel time and corresponding travel expense. In those cases, some difficult choices may be required regarding where to best place field technicians. In some logistically challenging situations, a service organization may find it more economically beneficial to utilize a local service vendor instead of the company's field technicians. It goes without saying, a cost/benefit analysis would be required to determine whether or not a decision to go with a third-party service provider would be financially prudent and operationally effective.

Many product companies have their own internal service organization, while other companies principally utilize authorized service providers for both in-warranty and out-of-warranty service. Generally, there is a correlation between a product company size and the internal service organization size and scope. Large product companies typically have extensive internal service organizations, while smaller companies have little or none. There are two basic reasons that is the case. First, service and support infrastructure require a substantial investment in people and spare parts inventory. Large companies will typically be able to generate compelling business justification for making those investments. Whereas, smaller companies, which typically have limited resources, simply cannot afford to make those same infrastructure investments.

The second reason has to do with physical coverage. If your company's products require on-site support, physical coverage can represent a significant logistical challenge. Let's say your company requires approximately 100 on-site technicians to support the amount of product in the installed base. Let's keep it simple and assume your company only sells and services products within the USA. In one scenario, let's assume the products are fairly widespread throughout the country, with virtually no concentrated areas. That basically means you'll need roughly two technicians per state, which will almost certainly be a costly logistical nightmare. The reason being, your technicians will spend most of what could otherwise be productive time traveling from one customer site to another. In a second scenario, let's consider a very different situation, in which your company's products are concentrated in a dozen major cities. That means you'll have roughly eight technicians in each major city, which would work much better from both a coverage and travel cost standpoint.

So, what do small/medium product companies do to provide on-site service to a relatively scattered installed base? Some will rely 100% on authorized service providers, while others might implement a hybrid support model. In the latter case, the company's internal service resources would likely support concentrated locations (such as urban areas), and the rest of the installed base would be supported by authorized service providers. However, I will tell you, the more service partners a company uses, the bigger will be the vendor and quality management challenges. My point being, you need to think long and hard about which support model best suits your company's needs and, more importantly, preserve your company's reputation for delivering quality service. Remember, from the client's perspective, how good or bad the delivered service quality reflects on your company, not your service provider. You cannot expect a client to disregard a bad service experience by giving them the following excuse. "It was one of our lesser quality service vendors that delivered the bad service, which we sincerely regret". The fact of the matter, your customer couldn't care less about your vendor management challenges. Ultimately, they will hold you, and only you, responsible for service quality.

Now let's talk about on-site support models that work best for large product companies that have an internal service organization. First of all, it's important to point out, these large company service organizations typically deal with somewhat different challenges than small/medium size companies. One of the principal differences, the latter will oftentimes heavily leverage third-party service providers to support their customers, since they typically cannot afford to invest in a services infrastructure. Hence, their primary focus is on vendor quality management and related cost control. Whereas, large companies that have invested heavily in an internal service infrastructure are generally more focused on continuous process improvements and corresponding cost reductions. Nevertheless, there are many situations in which large service organizations also leverage third-party service vendors. However, those vendors are oftentimes strictly used to augment internal service capability, which generally means servicing customers that are located in remote/rural areas.

In the old days, having a support technician walk into a customer site who was not a company employee was considered taboo. Times have changed for a number of reasons, which one of the most compelling reasons is competitive cost pressures. Let's face it. In many situations, having a 100% employee-based support solution will likely be more expensive than some other viable alternatives. Smart service organizations work very hard at institutionalizing the most cost-effective support solution possible that satisfactorily meets customer deliverable needs. Oftentimes, that means implementing a hybrid solution, which includes a mixture of internal and vendor provided services. That said, let's look at an example of a hybrid support solution.

Suppose you represent an internal service organization within a large product company. Suppose further that your company just sold a hardware solution to a major client for an entirely new data center. The product sale agreement also includes installation and extended support services. Assume further, there is a nearby service district office that has highly trained technicians that could easily handle the hardware installation and set-up effort. However, since those resources are highly trained, they also command relatively high salaries. Let's say their fully burdened average salary is $100K/year, which equates to roughly $50/hour. Assume further, there is a local third-party service company that has sufficiently trained resources that can handle the equipment installation and set-up for $25/hour. All things considered, a decision to go with the third-party company, instead of utilizing costly internal resources, is a no brainer. Incidentally, the corresponding software configuration, which is more complicated, would almost certainly be handled by the highly skilled internal resources. This is a classic example of a cost-effective hybrid solution.

There is one final comment I'd like to make regarding hybrid solutions similar the one just described, volume matters. Meaning, you wouldn't want to bring in external low-cost resources unless there is an appreciable amount of work for them to do, which would result in worthwhile savings. Otherwise, it would make more sense to simply have the local highly skilled resources handle all of the work.

Sensible Parts Replacement

Just as poor or inadequate diagnostics can lead to unnecessary on-site dispatch, once the field technician is on site, trial and error parts replacement represents another costly unwarranted practice. Generally speaking, the more knowledgeable and experienced field technicians will spend the necessary time and effort to hone in on a problem before proceeding with parts replacement. On the other hand, less experienced field technicians are more likely to approach the problem from a trial-and-error standpoint. Meaning, replace a part to see if it fixes the problem. If it doesn't, replace another part, etc.

This is a very costly approach that should be avoided. The primary reason, once you unseal and swap out a costly and particularly sensitive spare part, you cannot simply place it back in the good stock pile. Once the part is unsealed, you are forced to place it in the potential defective pile, which means it will need to be re-tested and re-sealed before it can be used again, even though the part may turn out to be in absolutely perfect condition. Bottom line, all of that unnecessary and costly parts re-testing and re-packaging could be avoided by using better trained and more experienced field technicians. Yes, using more highly skilled resources will result in higher labor cost. However, the incremental labor cost is likely to be lower than the cost of doing trial and error parts replacement.

Customer Assisted Repairs

Customer assisted repairs can cover a fairly broad spectrum, from a customer involvement standpoint. On one end of the spectrum, there are service providers that expect customers to handle much of the labor associated with repairs, even if the customer purchased an on-site service contract. I alluded to this type of situation earlier when I talked about my treadmill repair experience in Chapter 1. On the other end of the spectrum, there are clients who buy on-site service contracts that are unwilling to do anything to help the service provider. Even if it's something simple like resetting a switch or other relatively minor task. The position those customers take goes something like this. "I paid for an on-site service contract; therefore, expect the service provider to show up at my place of business to handle any/all problems/issues that may arise, no matter how small or insignificant."

The fact of the matter, in cases where service issues require minor attention, the customer is often better off handling the matter themselves. The reason being, unless there is a dedicated on-site technician assigned to the customer's building or campus, the customer will have to make arrangements to meet and escort the on-site technician. In which case, providing those accommodations often end up being more time consuming and costly for the customer (in terms of downtime) than simply handling the minor issue themselves.

As usual, settling on reasonable middle ground generally works best. In most cases, when customers and their service provider work cooperatively with one another, both parties stand to benefit. In some cases, a client's cooperation has to be bought with financial and/or reciprocity incentives. These incentives can be worthwhile for the client, especially if the defined tasks are painlessly simple. From the service provider's perspective, the agreed upon cost of customer incentives should be lower than the cost avoidance of dispatching a field technician for minor issues/problems.

Escalation Management

Finally, let's talk about escalation management, which is a function that is often embedded within the field operations organization. Obviously, not all service organizations can justify having an escalation management team. However, those that support mission critical clients typically do have them. And, the clients they support generally pay a premium price for the higher level service. In addition to rapid response, those clients receive special attention from the escalation manager who typically has priority access to executive managers that can make things happen quickly and without the usual bureaucracy. Simply put, escalation managers pave the way to quickly and efficiently resolve service issues, allowing customers to get up and running sooner than later.

Escalation Managers generally provide three services that are not made available to normal customers. First, deeper reach into the company's specialty resources, which may be required to resolve a particularly challenging problem. Sometimes that even includes individuals that are part of the product design and development team, who possess a deep understanding of product functionality and potential product performance issues. Second, escalation managers typically have better access to highly sought-after repair parts, whether those parts are coming from secondary markets or being pulled from the manufacturing build process. Obviously, the latter is generally met with considerable resistance from production managers, since the quantity of parts purchased is strictly intended for building product. Third, although escalation managers are oftentimes non-technical people, they do receive special training and have priority access to company resources, making them very effective at handling particularly time sensitive and critical service issues.

Chapter 4

Logistics Operations

When we consider the big ticket items in Customer Service & Support organizations, the two functions that immediately come to mind are Field Operations and Parts Logistics. From a financial standpoint, the former essentially just impacts the P&L because it is predominately a people cost function. Whereas, the latter impacts both the P&L and Balance Sheet.

From a P&L standpoint, Parts Logistics involve some people cost for such things as inventory planners, warehousing and distribution personnel, as well as expended parts cost consumed during repair activities. From a Balance Sheet standpoint, the single most significant Parts Logistics item is the value of spare parts inventory. Therefore, it's fair to say that Parts Logistics represents a substantial recurring cost, as well as a significant investment in company assets.

Furthermore, depending on the logistics business model the company utilizes, the financial implications can be far reaching from both a P&L and Balance Sheet standpoint. Incidentally, there is no such thing as one best logistics model. Meaning, each individual company's unique business needs will influence what is the best model for that company. There are three primary components to a Parts Logistics function, including inventory planning, warehousing, and distribution, which we are going to discuss in detail next.

Inventory Planning

Just as with Field Operations, which we discussed earlier, how well the front-end of Parts Logistics is handled can have a significant impact on both the business and the financial results. Basically, that means, how well inventory planning is handled represents a key element of success, which is precisely the reason a great deal of emphasis needs to be placed on this important function.

So, what constitutes good inventory planning? For the most part, placing orders for optimal quantities and in optimal frequencies. Furthermore, good planning means never running out of parts, or having too many parts on hand. Both situations (not enough or too many parts) can have equally consequential ramifications on either customer satisfaction and/or the company's finances. Incidentally, ordering strategies for low-cost expendable (or throughway) parts versus high cost repairable parts is quite different. We will discuss repairable parts in more detail later in the Product Repair section of the book.

Inventory planners typically consider several factors when they are placing parts orders, including the following: cost of the part, optimal order quantity, optimal order frequency, supplier availability, historical consumption rate, and more. When placing orders for low-cost parts, which suppliers are offering quantity discounts, the incremental cost of carrying some extra inventory is generally less that the volume discount offered by the supplier. Therefore, taking advantage of those volume discounts is oftentimes economically worthwhile. Next, let's look at an example of that specific scenario.

Let's assume you need 100 units of a particular low-cost part to fulfill foreseeable short-term future needs. Assume further, your supplier is offering a 20% discount on that particular part for order quantities of 500 or greater. So, the decision the inventory planner must make Is it more economically beneficial to take advantage or forego the quantity discount? The answer comes down to two factors. First, how long will it take for your company to consume 500 units of that particular part? Second, is there a potential obsolescence risk involved? In other words, possibly getting stuck with quantities the company will not be able to consume, which will subsequently have to be written off against the P&L. If the answer to the first question is, consumption of all 500 units will occur within one year. And, the answer to the second question is, there is no obsolescence risk. It would definitely be wise to take advantage of the quantity discount. On the other hand, if that large quantity is likely to take several years to consume, and/or present a moderate to high obsolescence risk, it would be unwise to place an order for 500 units.

Conversely, when an inventory planner is ordering high-cost parts, one of the primary considerations should be minimizing tying up too much working capital. In those cases, the inventory planner should order just enough quantities to meet short-term needs, plus maybe a few buffer units, just in case an extraordinary need should arise. For parts that are really expensive, planners should attempt to order them on a *just in time* basis. In other words, only order parts there is a known immediate need, and have them delivered just in time for use.

There is one other factor I'd like to discuss that inventory planners should consider, namely, supplier availability. When placing orders, inventory planners need to be aware of situations in which overall demand exceeds supply. Regardless of the part cost, if there is a supply shortage, it behooves the planner to order a larger quantity than might otherwise be considered *economic order quantity*. In most cases, there is no need to go completely overboard in these situations. In other words, the inventory planner might want to order three months instead of the normal one month supply. Ordering a one year supply would likely be considered going overboard. Finding a reasonable middle ground that does not have a significant adverse impact on working capital would be smartest approach. As mentioned earlier, there are other factors an inventory planner might rightfully consider when placing parts orders. Nevertheless, I believe we covered the most significant factors. Ultimately, I'd have to say, optimal order quantity and order frequency decisions represent the two most important factors inventory planners must consider when placing spare parts orders.

Warehousing and distribution

Depending on individual business needs, there are several different, equally effective spare parts warehousing and distribution strategies a company can adopt. One common strategy is having regional warehouses. Compared to a single national warehouse, a regional strategy would clearly result in more infrastructure investment and likely carrying more inventory. The reason for the latter, the more compartmentalized the inventory, the greater the total quantity required. On the other hand, parts that are regionally warehoused will be closer to your customers, which means they will arrive at the customer's site sooner and at a lower distribution cost. An example of the regional model might be having an East, Central, and West warehouse to cover the needs of USA based customers.

Another strategy is utilizing a *spoke and wheel* model, meaning a large distribution center located in the middle of the nation, which feeds several smaller regional warehouses located throughout the nation. Another strategy might be setting up a relatively small distribution center inside a national distribution company hub, for example the FEDEX hub in Memphis, Tennessee. Clearly, that space would be very expensive. Therefore, it should only be used for select critical parts. Another strategy might be stocking fast moving and common parts in field technicians' vans.

The last two suggestions would typically be considered complementary rather than primary distribution strategies. Meaning, they would be implemented along with one of the other above mentioned national, regional, or spoke and wheel strategies. Depending on the company's specific business needs, any one or combination of the above-mentioned strategies can be equally effective. Incidentally, from the field technician's perspective, the one thing that matters most is getting the parts he needs as quickly and hassle free as possible. And for customers, what matters most is getting up and running again as quickly as possible. In which case, field technicians and, in particular, customers don't care about the company's warehousing and distribution strategy. They just want the parts they need delivered to them on time and hassle free.

Inventory turns are typically one of the Key Performance Indicators (KPIs) used to measure warehousing effectivity. Cleary, the higher the turns, the more cost-effective the inventory and warehouse investment is considered. And of course, the opposite is true for low inventory turns. Keep in mind the total cost of carrying inventory is not just the aggregate value of the parts cost. One must also consider warehousing and distribution cost, as well as the cost of periodically taking physical inventories. That said, at this point, I'd like to share a couple of poor inventory management examples that I personally witnessed, which similar situations should be avoided.

One of the companies I worked for stocked printed service manuals for obsolete products, which took up approximately 1,000 square feet of shelving space in one of the company warehouses. We first noticed these manuals when we were doing the annual company-wide spare parts inventory. There were numerous broken and weathered boxes filled with old manuals, as well as individual manuals scattered everywhere on the shelving space. Based on the thick layer of dust covering everything in sight, it's safe to say those manuals had not been touched for years. Yet, the company still carried the inventory on its books at its original cost. Cleary, most, if not all, those manuals should have long been discarded and the corresponding inventory value written off. Keeping the manuals around contributed to inventory overvaluation, which is not a good thing, from a financial integrity standpoint. In addition, the manuals needlessly consumed valuable warehouse shelving space. Not smart, to say the least!

Another example of poor inventory management, which incidentally occurred at the same company, was carrying excess quantities of several parts that were clearly not moving. Essentially, these were parts for old desktop and laptop computers, which had long been declared obsolete. The parts consisted mostly of disk drives and laptop batteries, along with some motherboards and sundry other miscellaneous parts. As most of us who utilize technology products know, given the rapid advancements in technology and functionality of desktop and laptop computers, those products become obsolete rather quickly, Therefore, as older products are retired and replaced with new products, the need for old computer parts will drop dramatically and eventually cease. Furthermore, modern-day desktops and laptops cost only a fraction of what they used to cost a few years back. Therefore, it is not unusual for parts like old motherboards to be valued at a cost greater than the entire value of a new laptop or desktop computer.

Carrying those old motherboards, disk drives, and laptop batteries at their original cost, combined with the fact those parts would likely never be used, contributed to overstated inventory valuation. Just as with the obsolete service manuals mentioned above, the evidence of non-movement was obvious. All you needed to do is observe the undisturbed, thick layer of dust covering those parts. Here again, those parts should have long been discarded and the corresponding inventory value written off. As with most business management decisions, there is almost always an element of common sense that comes into play. Inventory management decisions are no exception. Clearly, something should have been done long ago in both described situations. Incidentally, if these matters were intentionally ignored by the responsible managers, that would have been considered inexcusable behavior, which would have certainly justified consequential disciplinary action.

Chapter 5

Repair and Refurbishment Operations

Product Repair Centers are very different from Product Return & Refurbishment Centers. The former typically provides two types of services. The first is repairing defective whole units that are sent in by customers for *repair and return* service. The second is component repair for such things as computer mother boards, which go back into good inventory after being repaired. Although it's relatively uncommon, some customers send in product components for repair and return service. By and large, the principal source of component repair parts is defective inventory bins. Those defective components usually come from repair service swap outs.

Product Return & Refurbishment Centers strictly deal with defective whole units that are either returned for customer credit or swapped for a refurbished or new replacement unit. Generally, the company's Dead on Arrival (DOA) policy will dictate whether the customer receives a refurbished or new replacement unit. More on this later when we get into the details.

Product Repair Centers

As mentioned above, Product Repair Centers generally deal with one or both of the following, repair and return of customer owned whole units and/or repair of defective product components. With regard to defective whole units, some product companies will only offer repair and return service during and after the warranty period. In other words, customers are not given the option of swapping out a defective unit for a refurbished unit. The one exception is DOAs, which are commonly swapped out for new units during the so called *DOA period*, which is typically 30 days after product receipt (more on DOAs later). Getting back to repair and returns, some customers prefer that service over refurbished swaps. The simple reason, they like the idea of getting back a unit they know received proper care, instead of a refurbished unit that may have previously been overused or neglected proper care.

With regard to defective component repairs, for the most part, they represent defective swap outs that are repaired and placed back into good inventory. There are some situations in which customers send in defective components for repair and return service; but, that's more so the exception that the rule.

For varying business reasons, which I would say have mostly to do with cost and/or quality control concerns, companies will often set up their own in-house repair center. Whereas, other companies outsource repair because they either do not want to deal with core business distractions, or they believe it's more cost-effective to outsource the repair work.

In addition to the repair choices already described, some companies will allow third-party service companies and/or product resellers to handle repairs. In these situations, I am not referring to outsourcing the repair work. Instead, I'm talking about allowing independent for profit companies to directly handle repairs with customers. In which case, product repair training and certification are absolutely essential to ensure repairs are done in accordance with the product company's guidelines. Furthermore, those repairs have to continuously be monitored for quality assurance, which can be done through a customer survey or reporting process.

Otherwise, unmanaged poor quality service will reflect badly on both the service provide and the product company for allowing poor quality service providers to directly handle the repairs.

At this point, I'd like to talk about repairable versus expendable classification, which is used to distinguish defective products that are sent to repair centers for rework versus products that are deemed throwaways. Although this classification can apply to both finished goods and spare parts, for our discussion we're going to strictly focus on the latter. There are two principal criteria used to determine whether a spare part is deemed repairable. First and foremost, is the spare part serviceable? In other words, can a repair technician effectively diagnose and replace sub-components that are built into the spare part? Second, will the repair be cost-effective? In other words, will it be economically worthwhile to actually do the repair? Let's consider a couple of examples.

Most computer motherboards are deemed repairable for the following reasons: they are usually easily removable from the whole unit; the subcomponents on the board are visible and accessible; and it is generally less expensive to repair than replace a motherboard. On the other hand, although disk drives are moderately expensive components that are easy to remove from the computer, they are deemed expendable. The principal reason, they are sealed units that are virtually impossible to repair. To be clear, I am not talking about data recovery from a disk drive, which can typically be done as long as you're willing to spend an outrageous amount of money to do so. A lesson to the wise, be sure to routinely back up your files, which is safer and considerably less expensive than having to deal with costly data recovery.

Incidentally, leveraging the services of independent repair companies may well be more cost-effective than companies doing their own repairs. Don't fall into the trap that internal is always better. Yes, a repair vendor will require management oversight. And yes, quality control is certainly a potential risk factor. However, in many situations, going with an independent repair vendor may turn out to be the better choice from an economic standpoint.

There is one final point I'd like to make regarding repair cost. Just because it may have been sensible and cost-effective to classify a particular spare part as repairable at a given point in time, does not mean the classification should stand indefinitely. Since I mentioned motherboards earlier, let's take a closer look at them from a repair decision standpoint. A couple decades ago, when everyday desktop and laptop computers were commonly priced at $2K - $3K, major components like motherboards were also very costly. Therefore, it made economic sense to repair those components. Now that low-end desktop and laptop computers have become commoditized, and can be purchased for a fraction of the old computer prices (let's say approximately $500 for a low-end computer), whether or not a motherboard should be deemed repairable has become a more difficult decision.

For discussion purposes, let's assume the average low-end computer motherboard cost $200, which represents approximately 40% of the computer price. When you consider the handling, testing and actual repair cost that would be involved, is it sensible to classify those motherboards as repairable? Maybe it is, or maybe it isn't. But surely, the cost of repair versus replacement are much closer together, potentially swaying the decision maker to go the other way and classify those motherboards as expendable. The underlining point, as products evolve, so too must repair strategies be reevaluated and potentially changed. The danger with blindly continuing to do what you've always done is almost guaranteed to eventually adversely affect the company's bottom line.

Product Return & Refurbishment Centers

A Product Return & Refurbishment Center is typically centrally located within a nation. For example, in the USA, a company would likely set up a return and refurbishment center in one of the mid-nation Sothern states. There are two primary reasons that would make strategic sense. First, the cost of labor tends to be relatively lower in mid-USA, particularly the South. The other, freight cost will be lower, particularly for heavy or bulky items that normally travel by truck or rail. Nevertheless, these centers are commonly responsible for the following activities: receive defective returns; make refurb or scrap decision for each returned unit; refurbish worthwhile units; distribute refurbished units for warranty and/or contracted service exchange; and sell off excess refurbished units.

Ordinarily, these centers only deal with returned finished goods that come back to the manufacturer for one of the following reasons: normal product failure, dead on arrival, and, in some cases, buyer remorse. Before proceeding further, allow me to explain the difference between normal product failure and DOA. In most companies, DOA designation means the product either did not perform as intended, or simply did not work from the very beginning. Typically, a product is deemed DOA if it fails within the first 30 days of product receipt. All other returns, except buyer remorse, which typically receive a refund, are treated as normal product failures. The distinction between the two return categories is important because DOAs are replaced with a new product;

whereas, all other defective returns are replaced with a refurbished product. As you might imagine, from a customer's point of view, there is a huge difference between getting a new versus refurbished replacement product. Therefore, it is not unusual for customer service representatives who deal with these matters to get some push back from customers who firmly believe their individual circumstance warrants new product replacement.

Although these return and refurbishment centers are unquestionably established with good intentions, they sometimes get out of control and largely turn into scrap centers. That is especially true for centers that are managed by people with unhealthy hoarding mentality. You know the type of individuals I am referring. Just like some homeowners who are afflicted with compulsive hoarding disorder, these individuals believe there will always be some use for the *junk* they are keeping around. By junk I mean multiple piles of product carcasses and left over components from cannibalized units that will most likely never be used. The fact of the matter, the cost of tying up warehouse space is probably far greater than the salvageable value of those junk piles. On the other hand, successfully run centers will strictly adhere to documented processes and disposition guidelines, as well as retain only pre-defined maximum levels of both defective and refurbished inventory. Incidentally, refurbishment only makes sense for relatively high-cost product. In most cases, companies are better off disposing low-cost defective returns because they are simply not worth the handling and refurbishing cost.

Aside from the potential issues and challenges just described, whether or not it makes sense to continue refurbishing various product models must continually be reevaluated. My point being, as the cost of manufactured product changes, so too must refurbishing cost be kept in line. Meaning, a product that was previously designated as worthwhile refurbishing when the cost/price was higher, may no longer be worthwhile handling and refurbishing. Designation changes are particularly common for new technology products that subsequently become commoditized.

Chapter 6

Managing CSS Overhead Functions

Too much overhead can be detrimental to an organization, particularly from a profitability standpoint. That is true for a company in its entirety, as well as organizations or business units within a company, such as Customer Service & Support. There are several overhead functions that are typically included in a CSS organization. The three most common include: Business Operations, Business Analysis, and in global businesses a Global Management Function. We are going to broadly discuss the responsibilities of each of these functions, with particular emphasis on whether or not all of the individuals in those functions are truly necessary and justifiable on the basis of return value.

Business Operations

Business Operations is an overhead function that exists in most major organizations or business units. They are typically responsible for the following: creating and updating business processes and procedures, monitoring and reporting key performance indicators, administering customer satisfaction surveys, and a host of other administrative duties. Oftentimes, Business Operations also becomes the *dumping ground* for undesirable admin work, which is offloaded by the other workgroups within the organization or business unit.

As the saying goes, "give someone a crutch and they will come to permanently depend on it." Meaning, once another workgroup has handed off admin work to Business Ops, good luck trying to give it back to the original owner. In business, undesirable admin work is a bit like a hot potato. No one wants to get stuck holding it. Also, when offloading admin work is permitted by management, it will generally stifle business process improvements. Why, you might ask? Because there is no incentive for the original owner to improve processes if they can simply unload undesirable work.

So, how do you effectively address a situation like the one just described? In the first place, don't allow admin work to be easily offloaded. The fact of the matter, if the owner of the admin work has no skin in the game, you should expect the undesirable behavior to continue in the future. The simple reason, the owner has nothing to lose and everything to gain from a workload standpoint. The best way to control this behavior is by requiring the workgroup that is seeking help to give something back to Business Ops. In business, one of the best ways to handle that is through the so-called *cost relief process.* In other words, cross charge the workgroup cost center that is receiving support, and credit the Business Ops cost center for the cost incurred providing the support. That way, you are infusing some pain (accountability) into the process, which is almost guaranteed to result in more responsible future behavior. On the other hand, giving those workgroups a pass, by allowing them to offload undesirable admin work without consequences, is simply not smart business.

Business Analysis

Unlike Business Operations, standalone Business Analysis functions are relatively less common. In many cases, business analysis is handled by Business Operations. Nevertheless, it's fair to say, somewhere within the organization, business analysis undoubtedly does occur. It may involve such things as:

analyzing what is happening in the marketplace, what competitors are doing, volume and/or profitability analysis for a particular client(s), etc.

Broadly speaking, I would characterize Business Analysis as a function that is focused on improving business processes and profitability, which is oftentimes done hand and hand with the Finance organization. Incidentally, there is no one best way of integrating business analysis into an organizational structure. It's simply a matter of preference and what management believes will work best in their individual circumstance. That said, I will tell you from personal experience, when a dedicated team of highly qualified and experienced analysts is justifiable, they can often work wonders to improve business processes and profitability.

There are two important factors that will influence success in a standalone Business Analysis team. First, the team manager must be a formidable member of the senior management staff. The reason being, if the function is buried elsewhere within the organization, it will likely not receive sufficient senior management attention to be successful. The second factor, team members must be willing to embrace the notion of self-dissolving. Meaning, if and when their value dwindles below their carrying cost, they must be willing to let go instead of struggling to hang on to simply protect their jobs. That is particularly true for the team manager, who sets the example for the rest of the team. Incidentally, if the team is eventually dissolved or, more likely, reduced in size, there are almost always other positions available elsewhere within the company for proven high performance individuals.

Allow me to share a real-life example of how a relatively small high performance business analysis team actually functioned, which, incidentally, I was a member. The team was led by a relentless no nonsense manager, and team members were empowered to do whatever was reasonably possible to improve business performance and profitability. Of course, that did not mean running around *willy-nilly* throughout the organization we supported creating angst and disruption. We definitely worked within a pre-defined framework and regulated guidelines. Furthermore, the projects we tackled were prioritized along with business management involvement and support. In other words, we made sure invested parties were *all in* before we tackled a project.

Since this team supported a relatively new business unit that was struggling with profitability challenges, our primary focus was in the following three areas. First, generate volume and statistical analysis reports regarding key aspects of the business, including accompanying customer level details. Second, identify troubled areas in the business, in particular unprofitable contracted deals. The analytical process usually started with a deep data dive, often down to transaction level detail, followed by the development and execution of short-term and/or long-term improvement plans. In some cases that led to changing business processes, and in a few other cases led to spearheading business policy changes. And finally, our third focus was developing tools and processes that improved the way business was managed. For example, we created and rolled out an intuitive and integrated contracted deal forecasting tool to improve a business process that was clearly lacking.

There were four things about this particular team that made it effective. One, there was a singular overarching focus, namely, improving profitability. Two, the team consisted of business-savvy and knowledgeable individuals who possessed a great deal of operations and/or financial management experience, and were well respected by the management team. Three, the team was fully empowered to do whatever was deemed appropriate and necessary to improve financial performance. And four, the team was led by a no nonsense manager that was part of the BU senior management team.

If a high impact team like the one described can be effectively integrated into a struggling company or BU you are involved, there is a high probability that team will generate worthwhile results. However, it is absolutely essential team members be empowered and given the required latitude to be successful. To be clear, just because this particular set-up worked well for us does not mean it's the only viable organizational solution. There are other equally effective ways of integrating business analysis into a company or BU. However, there are three fundamental ingredients that must minimally be present to be successful, including: crystal clear focus, high quality analysts, and management support. Without any of those basic ingredients, the chance of succeeding is dramatically reduced.

Now I'd like to talk about a potential downside of business analysis, something commonly referred to as *analysis paralysis.* The fundamental question that must always be asked about the analysis. When is enough enough? The answer will generally depend on the trade-off value of pursuing deeper level questions and answers. Sometimes it's reasonable to just scratch the surface to get the required answer. Other times, the business needs to ascertain a deeper understanding beyond a rudimentary answer. In which case, it may well be worthwhile pursuing progressively deeper level questions and answers. On the other hand, here is what unfortunately often happens in business. You are working for a particularly anal-retentive manager that has an obsession for details. Even though there is no legitimate business reason to analyze additional details, your manager will have you drilling down to the center of the universe (so to speak) seeking unjustifiable answers simply to satisfy his eccentric needs. That is a classic example of analysis paralysis. In other words, expending a great deal more unjustifiable time and effort pursuing answers that are totally unnecessary. Following is a real-life analysis paralysis example that I would like to share with you.

Before we get into the example details, I'd like to state that I wholeheartedly believe in business analysis, and buy into the basic notion of data driven decision making. However, in this particular case, I want to illustrate how easy it is to go completely overboard, effectively resulting in nothing more than a lengthy wheel spinning exercise. Along with one of my peers, we were directed to go through an analytical exercise, which had to do with a particular business function. Just as with most other large companies, we ran our business on robust business application systems, which meant we had an incredible amount of data available at our fingertips. Our mission was to turn a specific data set into useful information that could be leveraged to make better informed business decisions in the future. The details of the analytical exercise are not important. I'm strictly focusing on the process and the duration of this exercise.

Over a period of three months, the two of us sliced and diced the same data set numerous different ways, attempting to establish a cause-and-effect relationship among the various data elements. To be clear, I'm not talking about a full-time three-month project. This was one of several projects the two of us were handling at that time, which consumed approximately 20% of our collective time during that period. Although my associate and I believe that we arrived at a few reasonable conclusions from analyzing the data, our manager was never satisfied. One after another, our conclusions were rejected until a final decision was made by our manager to abandon the project.

I am not going to be judgmental here and say we were right and our manager was wrong or vice versa. However, I will say, this exercise took much too long and wasted many precious cycles, which, in the final analysis, accomplished absolutely nothing. In retrospect, our time could have clearly been spent on doing something more useful. Fundamentally, once an analytical exercise is brought to a reasonable conclusion, it should be deemed complete and the people involved should move on to the next project. Unfortunately, an anal-retentive manager will often decide otherwise. Meaning, he will require the analysts to continue digging wider and deeper for no apparent reason other than satisfying his own curiosity. Clearly this is wasteful behavior that must somehow be contained in business, and acted on by the manager's superior to stop it!

Global Functions

Businesses that are limited to national or local geographical scope do not have to deal with the global issues and challenges I am about to describe. Lucky for them! Whereas, in global companies, there are typically overarching global management functions. So, the question becomes, how much authority should those global management functions have? Let's consider a high-tech company that has three Product BUs and a horizontal CSS BU. Each of those BUs is led by an executive manager that is responsible for all aspects of their respective business unit, including the WW BU P&L. Reporting to each BU executive manager are WW region managers, which typically consists of an Americas, EMEA (Europe and Middle East), and Asia manager, who have P&L responsibility for their respective region. Also reporting to the BU executive are global function managers. So, that begs the following question. What exactly are the global function managers responsible? Also, do they also have P&L responsibility? Let's hold off answering those questions until we have taken a detailed look at a CSS WW BU.

Based on what has already been discussed, the CSS WW BU executive manager would have three WW region managers reporting to him, including one for the Americas, EMEA and Asia regions. In addition, he would have global function managers reporting to him, such as global delivery, etc. Generally speaking, the principal responsibility of those global function managers is to ensure global consistency in the manner in which CSS deals with customers, in particular WW customers. Therefore, those functions essentially represent policy and procedure organizations rather than P&L owners. The *real* P&L owners are the WW region managers. The problem that almost invariably arises over time, the global function managers get increasingly involved in the day-to-day WW region activities, including P&L management. That is precisely when contention between the WW region managers and the global function managers occurs. The simple reason, whenever you have two managers believing they are responsible for the same P&L, there is sure to be contention. My advice, don't allow this type of overlapping responsibility to occur because it will surely result in counterproductive behavior.

I am not suggesting global functions do not serve a useful purpose. Of course, they do. However, sometimes they simply get in the way. Let's face it, most business is done locally, meaning within a given region/country. Generally speaking, it's the region/country manager who is responsible for the local business, the people, and the corresponding P&L. Therefore, allowing the global functions to meddle too deeply in region/country business affairs is simply not a smart. Incidentally, as we all know, meddling is done by people. Therefore, the more people there are in a global function organization, the more meddling you should expect to occur.

At this point, I'd like to share a recent real-life example of a global function that morphed and grew disproportionate to the rest of the business unit. In this case, I am referring to the Global Delivery function. Previously, Global Delivery was reasonably staffed and limited to providing region/country oversight, which is precisely what they should have continued doing. Instead, they increasingly meddled in region/country affairs. Here are how things evolved in this particular case. Each year we created the annual region/country budgets, there was an ever-growing cost allocation to the P&Ls for the Global Delivery function. Meanwhile, all the region/country organizations, including the one I worked, were doing everything reasonably possible to preserve or improve gross margin. In other words, protect the portion of the P&L we had direct control.

On the other hand, allocated cost below the gross margin line kept growing each year, effectively eroding any margin gain the region/country managers might have been able to generate. Most of the allocated overhead cost increase was coming from a single organization. You guessed it, Global Delivery. Meanwhile, there was no noticeable incremental value coming back to the BU for the additional overhead cost. As a matter of fact, the opposite was occurring (more on this in a few moments). Keep in mind, in most global companies it's the BU global executive staff that is ultimately responsible for the final worldwide BU budget. The region/country managers can complain about elements of the P&L they don't like, such as ever-growing revenue challenges and overhead allocations. But, those complaints are almost sure to fall on deaf ears. In the public sector, that would be like the State Governments telling the Federal Government they will not accept financial responsibility for Federal mandates. Good luck with that!

What was even worse about this situation, we constantly felt the ever-growing presents of Global Delivery. In other words, they were increasingly meddling in region/country business affairs, which was clearly outside their original mandate. Before we knew it, Global Delivery personnel became involved in contracted deal reviews, as well as demand strict monthly reporting formatting and more. To a large extent, their involvement in deal reviews represented nothing more than unnecessary interference, coupled with more questions the account managers needed to answer, which also meant more follow-up work would have to be done. The reporting requirements can best be described as nothing more than satisfying Global Delivery staff formatting preference. The actual data in those reports were essentially the same as pre-existing region/country reports. A wise business associate of mine appropriately characterized much of Global Delivery involvement and demands as more so motion than value add.

Allow me to share an example of what I am referring. But, first I'd like to say that preparing for account reviews takes a great deal of precious time away from the account manager, whose primary responsibility is overseeing everyday client needs. At the region/country level, account reviews were done in accordance with pre-defined parameters and cadence guidelines, which were principally based on the size of the gap between plan versus actual financial results. Simply put, the greater the gap, the more frequent the required contracted deal reviews. For especially troubled accounts, reviews were done on a monthly or quarterly basis. Accounts that were moderately off from plan were reviewed on a half year basis. And accounts that were achieving or exceeding plan were reviewed once/year.

Although not perfect, the region/country account reviews were reasonably effective. However, that did not matter to Global Delivery management who began requesting their own reviews, subjecting the same account managers to more unnecessary work. By the way, the work does not end with preparing and delivering additional account reviews. Invariably, there were several performance related questions asked by the global team, which required additional analysis and follow-up responses. There is no polite way to say this. Those reviews essentially represented wasted cycles that did nothing to address meaningful performance issues, which were not already being addressed as a result of the region/country reviews. Meaning, the additional reviews and corresponding follow-up work amounted to nothing more than satisfying global management curiosity. Long story short, we finally convinced the global team to join the region/country reviews instead of hosting their own, which they eventually reluctantly agreed.

I could share several other examples, but will refrain from doing so. In the final analysis, the BU Global Function we just discussed impacted the region/country businesses in the following manner. First, they burdened the Region/Country P&Ls with ever-growing cost allocation. Second, they increasingly meddled in region/country business affairs. Third, they consumed precious region/country resource cycles on matters that did nothing to truly advance the business. Bottom line, Global Functions can certainly contribute to a BU and overall company success, as long as they remain focused on establishing and maintaining guidelines that ensure global consistency in the manner in which region/country businesses operate and deliver client services. Ultimately, these functions need to be held accountable for bringing tangible value back to the organization, rather than growing at will.

Chapter 7

Managing Other Aspects of CSS Businesses

Equally important to cost effectively managing the internal organization, CSS businesses must also manage other critical elements of their business, including clients, vendors, and assets. We're going to discuss each of these three elements in more detail shortly. In the meantime, it's important to be mindful, the manner in which each element is managed will undoubtedly have P&L implications. With regard to assets, which for CSS businesses consists mostly of spare parts inventory, how effectively those assets are managed will also have Balance Sheet implications. Incidentally, since this book is primarily focused on maximizing profitability, discussion regarding the Balance Sheet will be relatively limited.

Managing Clients

The level of service and support customers receive from a CSS organization depends on whether they are covered under standard warranty or a billable service contract. Generally speaking, contracted services include more coverage than standard warranty. The principal reason, contract customers buy the service level they need; whereas, warranty customers receive the service level product companies are willing to cover, which is typically minimal.

The issues and challenges CSS organizations typically face with warranty customers have mostly to do with what's covered under standard warranty and challenges regarding the warranty coverage period. Let me give you an example of the latter, which, incidentally, commonly occurs when a product fails shortly after the warranty period expires. These customers will often argue that it's unfair to have the warranty period begin on the date the product is shipped (or received). Furthermore, they will argue the product they purchased was not made operational until long after it was received. Depending on how convincing a case the customer makes, may result in the customer service rep allowing some leeway. But, I must warn you, the amount of discretion customer service reps have in this regard is usually limited, which is the reason customers will often request the matter be escalated to a supervisor or manager.

Another common challenge from warranty customers is whether or not a defective product should be treated as DOA. You may recall, we talked about DOAs earlier. The argument here simply comes down to whether the customer receives a refurbished or new replacement unit. Customers will often argue the product they purchased was operational for a short period of time before it failed. In other words, the product sat idle for several weeks/months beforehand. Therefore, they should receive a new (rather than refurbished) replacement unit. Here again, it may be reasonable for the company to allow a few exceptions. But, they must be careful not to be overly graceful in these matters.

The final example of a warranty customer issue I will provide has to do with return freight cost. Although standard warranty terms and conditions will often spell out that customers are responsible for return freight, some customers will push back on this matter, especially if the return involves costly freight. Moreover, there are many situations in which warranty coverage is limited to repair and return support, as opposed to exchange. In those cases, customers may request packaging material because they threw out the original packaging. If those requests are honored, that would mean incurring additional cost for packaging material and freight. Of course, the other option would be having the customer pay for the packaging and freight, which I presume is more common, but not without resistance from many of those customers.

Bottom line, you are apt to encounter any/all of the above-mentioned issues and challenges and more with warranty customers. In which case, on one end of the spectrum, the service organization could take the position of strictly adhering to warranty terms and conditions, even though that may upset some customers. On the other end of the spectrum, there are service organizations that tout the noble notion of wanting to delight their customers, which can easily turn into a very expensive proposition. In my opinion, neither of those two extremes is the right thing to do. Instead, finding a reasonable middle ground will almost always work best, which helps contain cost and satisfy a reasonable number of customers who are experiencing extraordinary circumstances.

Issues and challenges service organizations are apt to encounter with contract customers are generally different from those encountered with warranty customer. One of those big issues is response versus resolution time, which is particularly important to customers who are running critical business applications on equipment that is covered by a service contract. While some customers acknowledge and accept the distinction between response and resolution time, other customers either don't understand or are simply unwilling to accept the fact there is a difference. In which case, a customer that is anxiously awaiting a service incident resolution may say something like this. "I have been waiting over 24 hours for you to fix my problem." To which the customer service rep may respond as follows. "Our field technician responded (arrived at your site) within eight hours, as required by the service contract. However, he encountered issues that are likely going to take two days to resolve." Who's right and who's wrong in this case? Cleary the customer service rep is right because the technician responded within eight hours. Try telling that to a customer who is distraught because his business is going to be down for two days instead of eight hours.

Another common issue with contract customers has to do with customer assisted repairs. You may recall, we talked about customer assisted repairs earlier. In these situations, some customers may take the following position. "I am paying for on-site service; therefore, I expect an on-site technician to show up at my door whenever a service issue arises, no matter how small or insignificant it may be." To which the customer service rep may respond as follows. "The contract clearly states the customer is responsible for handling minor issues that do not require an on-site technician." Here again, who's right and who's wrong in this case? Once again, the customer service rep is right. Nevertheless, should the service organization give in on some these issues? I would say only in contested issues that could have potentially serious customer relationship implications.

Just as with warranty customers, there is a myriad of issues and challenges you are apt to encounter with contract customers, which you could respond in similarly extreme fashion. That is, either strictly adhere to contract terms and conditions, or bend over backwards for your customers because your motto is *delighting customers*. Remember, delight generally comes with an extraordinary cost tag. So, the question becomes, can you really afford to delight your customers? Being a little lenient in justifiably reasonable situations can be good for business, while bending over backward is definitely the wrong thing to do.

And finally, let's talk about the issues and challenges service organizations are apt to encounter with customers who have signed big deal contracts, which are often referred to as strategic accounts. Let's decode what a strategic account really means from a financial perspective. It usually means the customer receives favorable pricing, which in turn translates to relatively low margins, which in turn translates to having little wiggle room to remain on the positive side of margin neutrality. Nevertheless, when one of these big deals is signed, everyone is happy, right? Maybe!

Here's the thing about strategic clients. They typically represent large national or global companies who are masters at vendor management, as well as making lots of noise. That is to say, routinely escalate matters (required or not), which quickly find their way to the service organization executive sponsor. In other words, the person that is responsible for the high-level relationship with the client. When that happens, everyone involved with the client starts jumping through hoops to address matters that would otherwise have been considered routine, and more efficiently handled through normal business processes. Talk about unnecessary and costly angst!

Incidentally, these same strategic accounts are typically assigned a dedicated account manager, and in some cases a dedicated account team, which translates to higher than normal support cost. Furthermore, since relationship management with these clients is critically important, service providers are often lenient when it comes to billing for a *little* extra work the customer requests. Although being a little lenient in select circumstances makes for good business, being overly lenient is definitely bad for business. By the way, I am not suggesting strategic accounts are bad for business. However, I am stating they must be thoughtfully managed. Bottom line, it's important to mindful, business that contributes positively to the top line is only good if it does the same to the bottom line. Unprofitable or marginally profitable revenue is never good for business.

Managing Vendors

CSS organizations generally engage with several different types of vendors. For example, they do business with spare parts supply vendors, on-site service vendors, repair vendors, warehousing and distribution vendors, etc. For all intents and purposes, virtually everything that is done by internal CSS resources can be outsourced to vendors. Nevertheless, besides spare parts supply vendors, I would say the most common type of vendor CSS organizations do business is on-site service providers, which are either used to augment internal service capability or in lieu of internal service. When on-site service is provided by a third-party company, there should always be a written agreement between CSS and the vendor regarding end-client deliverables. Furthermore, if there are non-performance penalties associated with end-client deliverables, those same penalties must be incorporated into the vendor agreement.

Managing Assets

Just as with any other business unit, depending on the level of independence it has, a CSS organization could very well deal with a variety of assets, including accounts receivable, inventory, fixed assets (such as buildings), etc. Nevertheless, it's fair to say, the most significant asset CSS organizations are typically responsible is spare parts inventory. Since we already discussed spare parts inventory management in a fair amount of detail in the Logistics chapter, I will limit additional comments to the following paragraph.

Every aspect of spare parts inventory management is critically important from both a P&L and Balance Sheet standpoint. It starts with smart inventory planning, meaning not having too much or too little inventory on hand. Next comes the physical management of inventory. Keeping accurate perpetual inventory records is critically important, as is taking annual physical inventory and doing reconciliations of actual to perpetual inventory balances. Also crucial is taking timely action to address excess and/or obsolete inventory. Basically, if there is no realistic plan demonstrating that on hand inventory will be consumed in the foreseeable future, the excess inventory should be written off. Waiting for something magical to happen that will consume those parts is nothing more than wishful thinking. Ignoring the problem is even worse, which in my opinion represents irresponsible management. Furthermore, the chosen spare parts warehousing and distribution strategy also has both P&L and Balance Sheet implications. It bears repeating, there is no one best warehousing and distribution strategy. It basically comes down to what strategy best serves the company and customer needs at a reasonable cost.

Chapter 8

CSS Business Application Systems

Besides standard business application systems that exist in most companies for such things as: sales order and distribution management, materials management, accounts receivable, accounts payable, procurement, etc., there are three critically important application systems that are required to support and manage a CSS business. First is a Contract Management and Billing System, which is principally used to manage service contracts and related billing. The second is a Field Service Management System, which is principally used to manage field technicians' repair activity. And third is a Call Management System, which is principally used to manage customer service and technical support calls. We are going to discuss all three systems in more detail shortly. In the meantime, I would like to briefly talk about business application systems in general.

In the old days, most business application systems operated independently from one another, even though actual business activity operated in a very much integrated fashion. Those independent systems were used to manage single tasks, such as: Sales Order Processing, Accounts Receivable, Accounts Payable, etc. Incidentally, in the *really* old days, business systems were not even integrated with the company's General Ledger. Meaning, business related financial transactions were not automatically posted to the General Ledger. Instead, summary reports generated from those systems represented the source data used to post accounting entries to the General Ledger each month. As time passed, those independent business systems became increasingly more integrated with the General Ledger. Meaning, most accounting entries were automatically posted to the General Ledger, while minimizing the need for manual journal entries to handle only the exceptions.

During the past couple of decades, independent business application systems have increasingly become a thing of the past. Instead, companies are increasingly implementing fully integrated business systems, commonly referred to as Enterprise Resource Planning (ERP) systems. Basically, that means essentially all business functions are systematically interconnected. For example, when a sales order is processed, that transaction will subsequently affect the following integrated business system modules in an automated fashion: order processing, billing, shipping, inventory, costing, and eventually the P&L. Without getting too much deeper into the details, suffice to say ERP systems such as SAP, have done wonders to systematically integrate businesses and streamline accounting. Furthermore, they have dramatically helped reduce manual accounting errors, since virtually all accounting postings are automated.

Next, we will talk about the three above-mentioned service business application systems. Although we will discuss these systems individually, it's important to be mindful, they would represent integrated modules in an ERP system. That said, let's start with the Contract Management and Billing System.

Contract Management and Billing System

Although Contract Management and Billing Systems are principally utilized to manage contracts and related billing, they do much more than those two basic functions. For example, the system database typically contains customer specific contract coverage data, by model and serial numbers. Hence, when a customer calls for service, the CSS support agent can validate whether or not the specific product the customer is calling about is covered under contract, as well as the service level that product is entitled.

The reporting features that are built into these systems are generally fairly robust. Meaning, there are a number of standard reports and countless ad hoc report views that can be generated from these systems. Generally speaking, any/all data that is posted to the system database, down to business transaction level detail, can be retrieved for reporting and analysis purposes. And of course, these systems almost always have automated feed capability into the General Ledger.

Despite the fact Contract Management and Billing Systems typically contain several other useful features, we will limit our discussion to just one more, namely, deferred revenue. Although monthly billing is a standard option, quarterly and/or annual billing options are also often made available for service contracts. For the service company, the upfront billing provides cash flow advantages. And for the client, it provides an opportunity to take advantage of a pre-payment discount, which is commonly offered with advanced billing options. Nevertheless, there are accounting regulations that dictate how the revenue reporting must be handled.

Generally accepted accounting principles require earned revenue and corresponding cost to be recognized in the same accounting period. Therefore, portions of the advanced billing must be treated as deferred revenue. The best way to demonstrate how deferred revenue and corresponding cost works is with an example. Let's assume a customer is billed $1,200 for a full year service contract. Even though the service company will benefit from a cash flow standpoint, they cannot recognize the entire billed amount as earned revenue. Instead, revenue must be recognized over a 12 month period at $100/month. Let's keep it simple and say the service company incurs approximately $75 cost each month to support that contract. That means the contract will generate $25 gross margin each month ($100 - $75). Incidentally, with regard to financial integrity, revenue and cost matching is one of the fundamental accounting principles all businesses must adhere.

Field Service Management System

Field Service Management Systems are principally used to dispatch and record on-site service activity. These systems are typically integrated with several other application systems (or ERP modules), such as: Contract Management and Billing, Human Resource Management, Inventory Management and, of course, the General Ledger. The repair data that is captured in Field Service Management Systems serve multiple reporting purposes, including:

1. Labor, parts and travel cross-charges to be made to the Product BUs.

2. Labor, parts and travel charges to be billed to T&M customers.

3. Assessment of individual field technician utilization.

4. Assessment of individual field office resource utilization.

5. Identify products that experience unusually high repair rates, which appropriate countermeasures can (should be) taken.

6. Identify customer environments that experience unusually high incidence rates, which appropriate countermeasures can (should be) taken.

Following is a list of primary data elements that are typically captured during on-site repair activities, and their uses:

1. Field technician name and job code:

> ➤ Used to calculate the repair incident labor cost. Noteworthy, these systems typically contain fully burdened labor rates by job code, which will be explained in more detail below.

2. Customer name and number:

> ➤ Used for customer level reporting and analysis.

3. Geographic region repair incident occurred:

> ➤ Used for regional reporting and analysis.

4. Product model and serial number:

> ➤ Used to validate service and support entitlement.

5. Repair start and stop time:

> ➤ Used to calculate repair labor cost.

6. Travel start and stop time, plus any related travel expenses:

> ➤ Used to calculate travel cost associated with repair incident.

7. Parts consumed in repair incident:

> ➤ Used to cross-charge Product BUs and bill T&M customers for parts consumption. Also used to reflect reduction in parts inventory balance.

The list of items and related uses I just described in not intended to be all inclusive. Nevertheless, the list does include the most common items that are captured, reported and analyzed from Field Service Management Systems.

As promised, let's now talk about fully burdened labor rates that are typically embedded in these systems. But, before we do, a few words about what is a fully burdened labor rate. Simply put, these labor rates include the following: hourly wage, fringe and other labor-related overhead, management overhead, and a utilization factor. In fact, the accuracy of the burdened labor rates is quite important. The reason being, actual hours worked multiplied by the fully burdened labor rate reflects the amount cross-charged to the Product BU or billed to T&M customers. Just so there is no misunderstanding, allow me to clarify an important point before discussing this matter further. From a total company P&L standpoint, these labor rates do *not* matter. The reason being, burdened labor rates are strictly created and used for cross-charge and billing purposes. In other words, customer and regional P&Ls are impacted by burdened labor rates; whereas, the total company P&L is not impacted. All of the above-mentioned burdened labor rate cost components find their way into the total company P&L through other direct cost posting means.

Now let's talk about how we arrive at fully burdened annual labor cost. We start with the average gross salary by job code. Let's assume the average salary for a particular job code is $80,000. To which we add 25% fringe plus 25% for other labor-related overhead, making the burdened gross salary $120,000. To that, let's add 12.5% management overhead, making the management burdened salary $135,000. As mentioned earlier, there is one additional item that must be considered when creating fully burdened labor rates, namely, a utilization factor. It's hardly reasonable to assume a service organization will realize 100% utilization from any given individual. In other words, achieve 100% productive time. The fact of the matter, there will be downtime for admin work, training, vacation, sick time, as well as unproductive bench time that needs to be factored into fully burdened labor rates. From my experience, I'd say a reasonable utilization assumption for field technicians in a CSS organization is roughly 65%, which is what we will use in the following example.

Finally, let's look at how fully burdened labor rates are calculated. Assuming 52 weeks and a 40-hour work week, there are 2,080 available hours in a year. Starting with the management burdened salary of $135,000 (calculated above), gives us an hourly labor rate of $64.90 ($135,000 / 2,080 hours). When we factor in the 65% utilization assumption, it reduces the total year available hours from 2,080 to 1,352. Therefore, the fully burdened labor rate that is entered into the Field Service Management System would be $99.85 ($135,000 / 1,352 hours).

Ideally, you would create several different labor rates, one for each job code. Within a particular job family, you might have three or more job codes. Let's assume the field technician job family has three job codes, including one for each of the following levels: L1, L2, and L3. Let's assume the annual management burdened salaries for those three job codes are $115,000, $135,000, and $155,000, respectively. Taking into consideration the 65% utilization factor would make the L1 fully burdened labor rate $85.06 ($115,000 / 1,352); the L2 rate $99.85 ($135,000 / 1,872); and L3 rate $114.64 ($155,000 / 1,872). That's the level of detail that needs to be considered when creating fully burdened labor rates that are built into Field Service Management Systems.

As you can see, we did not use actual employee salaries in our examples, which there is likely considerable variation from one employee to another in the same job code. Instead, for manageability reasons, we used the average salary for each job code. Granted, this approach does not produce 100% accurate labor rates. However, for the intended purpose, this method is sufficiently accurate, and certainly much less cumbersome than dealing with countless individual actual salaries. Some companies may take a slightly more or less granular approach creating fully burdened labor rates. Ultimately, as long as the guidelines and assumptions used are reasonable and consistent, the results should be sufficiently reliable.

Call Management System

Call Management Systems are principally used for call routing and capturing customer call-in information. In CSS businesses, these systems are primarily used in Customer Service and Technical Support Centers, which represent two major customer touch points. These systems typically come with, more or less, the following standard built-in functionalities:

1. Real-time dashboard monitoring, which serves several useful purposes, including:

    A. Call queue monitoring, which help managers make insightful resource distribution decisions. In other words, staff for call spikes and lulls.

    B. Monitoring individual customer service and technical support agent performance, regarding number of calls taken, average call duration, etc.

2. Call queue routing and prioritization, meaning getting calls into the right queue (whether that's a product line queue or else), as well as addressing calls based on assigned priority level.

3. Call recording capability, which is routinely done for legal and agent quality monitoring purposes. The latter provides a means for giving constructive call handling feedback to customer service and technical support agents.

4. Robust standard and ad hoc reporting capability, and more.

These systems go by different names, such as: Call Management Software, Contact Center Software, and Call Center Software. Furthermore, there are several software product companies that offer these systems, which some can be integrated with other company software, such as an ERP system, while others operate as standalone systems. Nevertheless, these systems are absolutely essential for CSS businesses to support both technical and non-technical customer needs and services.

Part II

Managing Human Resources

Chapter 9

Justifying Human Resources

Service businesses are largely people cost businesses. Therefore, how those people are justified, measured, and managed matters a great deal from a profitability perspective, which is the reason I devoted the entire second part of the book to the subject matter. First, we're going to talk about justification processes for existing, replacement and additional resources, each having their own unique challenges and one common shortcoming, namely, lacking process rigor. Unfortunately, many companies do not routinely apply sufficient rigor to human resource justification processes until it's too late. Meaning, they are experiencing financial difficulty, requiring them to tighten their hiring processes.

Instead of being reactive, which oftentimes means doing too little, too late to have *real* impact on the business, we're going to talk about ways to get in front of this challenge to avoid potential downstream consequences. Speaking from extensive personal experience, I can safely state that when companies are in reactive mode, the resource approval process is generally painfully slow. As a result, managers who are in desperate need of replacing critical resources, especially customer facing resources, suffer the greatest consequences. The reason being, delaying replacement of critical customer facing resources will often result in the inability to meet contracted deliverables, which is never a good thing. That is especially true when non-performance financial penalties are involved. Hence, the wise thing to do is treat requests for customer facing replacement resources with a greater sense of urgency.

Justifying Existing Resources

Unless a business is performing particularly poorly, existing resources are ordinarily not re-justified during the annual budgeting process. Instead, those resources are considered part of a baseline budget, which frankly speaking is unfortunate. The reason being, companies are not taking advantage of potential resource cost reduction opportunities that may exist. Typically, as businesses grow and change, so too change their resource requirements. There are numerous reasons resource requirements can change. For illustration purposes, we're going to talk about a couple of common reasons.

First, as a result of business growth, let's assume a company decides to migrate from several disparate business application systems to an integrated enterprise system like SAP. As you might imagine, for most companies this would represent a significant and costly undertaking. Accordingly, they would ultimately expect to yield some efficiency benefits from the investment, including a reduction of Information Technology (IT) resources. If you have ever been involved in a sizable enterprise business application system implementation, you know that they are typically long-term projects, which could easily take two or more years to fully implement. Companies that are implementing these systems usually bring in expert resources from a management consulting firm to guide them, and sometimes lead the system configuration and implementation effort. Furthermore, those companies are likely to assign select internal IT resources to the project, in order that those individuals are able to support both the system and user community after the system rollout.

Generally speaking, the integration of those resources works as follows. Throughout the configuration and implementation phases, select internal IT resources become seamlessly integrated with the consulting resources. Shortly after the system has been rolled out, the consultants move on, leaving only the internal IT resources to support the system and the user community. Since the new system functionality is invariably different from the old disparate systems, there is growing reliance on IT resources from the user community. And before you know it, IT resources are busy helping end-users execute business transactions, running reports, etc. Frankly, much of what occurs is nothing more than handholding (so to speak), until the users become more self-sufficient utilizing the new system.

Given this common development, the following question typically arises. What happened to the original plan of reducing internal IT resources after the new system is implemented? The answer is, activities such as running ad hoc reports, which end-users previously performed on their own, now require IT resource assistance to do the same on the new system. Also, what was considered routine business transactions in the old systems are now causing some users difficulty executing similar transactions on the new system, resulting in IT resources having to help those users. These challenges will eventually dissipate, but it may take the better part of a year before end-users become fully self-sufficient. In the meantime, management is caught squarely in the middle of a classic dilemma.

They could choose to play hardball and reduce the originally planned IT resources, but that would upset the user community. On the other hand, they could continue to have IT resources provide end-users hand holding assistance, but that would result in unbudgeted financial consequences. So, what should management do? The right answer is objectively analyzing the situation and take immediate action to minimize dependency on IT resources.

Let's assume management determines IT resources are spending approximately 25% of their time helping end-uses run reports and execute business transactions. In that case, the most likely course of action would be investing in end-user training, which will make them more self-sufficient and less reliant on IT resources sooner than later. Doing nothing is not a viable option. The reason being, as the saying goes, "provide someone a crutch and they will come to always depend on it." On the other hand, slowly wean the person off the crutch and see how quickly he starts walking on his own again. The same holds true for IT assistance. Meaning, the best approach is to identify and prioritize activities that are causing end-users difficulty, and systematically address those activities with targeted improvement initiatives.

Another common example of missed resource reduction opportunity occurs when business process improvements are implemented. Most companies continuously modify their internal processes to meet ever-changing business needs. Also, many companies routinely look for ways to make existing processes more efficient. The fact of the matter, streamlining business processes represents only partial success. Taking corresponding resource action is equally important. Unfortunately, many companies claim success when process improvements are implemented, and do not take the next logical step to reduce resources that are no longer needed. The reason being, many managers struggle with that next step. They naturally do not want their team members to be out of a job. But, here's the thing. Embracing those unpopular and difficult decisions when they present themselves can potentially circumvent having to deal with broader based resource decisions when the company's overall success or longevity may be on the line.

Just as new resources need to be justified, existing resources should also periodically be re-justified. I'm not suggesting companies adopt a zero-based budgeting process in order to contain non-essential resource cost. However, I am recommending companies periodically reevaluate resource needs, especially indirect resources. The basic reason, ensure the company continues to receive justifiable return value from those resources. The most effective way to do that is to periodically re-assess the need for the tasks indirect resources are performing, and objectively evaluate the impact to the business if those tasks were to cease. You may quickly come to realize that many tasks that were once considered vital to the business are no longer necessary. For example, on-going reporting and analysis that may have been implemented for a special need or circumstance that no longer requires constant monitoring.

Oftentimes, new reporting and/or analytical processes are instituted as a result of problems that have occurred in a business. As time passes and notable progress is made resolving those business issues, the reporting and analysis nevertheless routinely continue, even though management is no longer truly paying attention to the matter. So, what should management do in these situations? The first step, identify and eliminate non-essential tasks and consolidate the remaining tasks under fewer individuals. The second step, eliminate resources that are no longer needed. As previously stated, the latter step is not pleasant. In which case, some managers will shy away from taking that action. On the other hand, managers who are motivated to deliver improved performance are more likely to embrace those actions as an opportunity to positively impact the company's bottom line, as well as improve the likelihood of their own professional growth.

I'd like to make one additional comment regarding containment of existing resource cost. Given that people represent the lion's share of service cost, running a successful and profitable service business is a perpetual balancing act between resource cost management and maintaining desirable customer satisfaction levels. That said, although managers are paid to make business decisions, oftentimes it's the people on the ground, who work directly with customers, that know best. Therefore, my advice is to encourage those people to come forth with process and/or profit improvement ideas, and reward them for ideas that are implemented. It's amazing how many worthwhile ideas can come from individuals who are on the ground, especially ideas that make it possible for organizations to work smarter, faster, and cheaper without sacrificing customer satisfaction. The fact of the matter, besides his or her job skills, every person brings their brain to work every day. So, why not leverage everything they have to offer?

Justifying Replacement Resources

Except during unusually challenging business circumstances, most companies treat hiring of replacement resources as a foregone conclusion. Meaning, if there was good reason for having the position filled before it was vacated, there is good reason to backfill it now. Instead, management should look at every resource replacement as a potential cost reduction opportunity. Sometimes the position being vacated can be replaced with a partial resource. In other cases, management should consider doing the following. Evaluate all of the incumbent's activities and separate them into critical and non-critical categories. Eliminate non-critical activities, and either give the remaining activities to another existing resource or divide them amongst several resources who have available bandwidth.

In other situations, there may be an opportunity to replace the vacated position with a lower job level. Sometimes the existing job level is unduly influenced by the seniority and experience level of the incumbent, instead of the knowledge and skills truly required to do the job. In those cases, it would behoove the hiring manager to backfill the position with a lower level resource or maybe a new college hire. Either way, the work will get done at a lower cost, something managers should always be striving to achieve.

Incidentally, although new college hires typically do not possess a significant amount of experience coming into a new position, they tend to learn and grow rapidly. In many cases, they will give their all in return for being given an employment opportunity. Of course, the same may be true for motivated existing employees who are given advancement opportunities. Nevertheless, there are a number of different approaches the hiring manager can potentially take advantage to reduce replacement resource cost. Bottom line, each situation should be approached with the following two things in mind. Adopt the best solution that fulfills *essential* business needs, and takes advantage of any potential cost reduction opportunities that may exist.

On the other hand, there are situations in which time sensitive client support replacement decisions should be made that are not. Delays could be due to a company's *one size fits all* replacement policy, or a hiring approval manager deliberately dragging his heels. Regardless of the reasons for delays, the results are never good and oftentimes consequential. Sure, a service provider may save some money during the time the replacement position is left vacant, but at what cost? I have been on the receiving end of delayed resource replacement decisions. And, can tell you, it's particularly frustrating for an account manager or delivery manager that is stuck in the middle. The reason being, they are hamstrung by poor internal policies or management practices, while still being expected to meet customer deliverables without sufficient resources.

The fact of the matter, customers don't care about the service provider's internal policies and processes. All they care about is ensuring the service provider meets their delivery obligations. When deliverables are not met, there will be consequences. In some cases, it may result in something relatively minor, such as a temporarily dissatisfied customer. In other cases, it could result in something more serious such as a non-performance financial penalty. The point being, customers have a number of different options they can exercise when a service provider is not delivering on their promise. In which case, resource shortages will certainly add to non-performance risk.

The bottom line, resource replacement processes must be sufficiently flexible to meet varying business needs. Whenever a *one size fits all* process is implemented, there will invariably be resulting consequential issues and challenges. Generally speaking, replacing direct labor resources, especially people who are responsible for customer deliverables, need to be treated with a greater sense of urgency than replacing indirect resources. On the other hand, every resource replacement (especially indirect resources) should be viewed as a potential cost reduction opportunity.

Justifying Additional Resources

Justification for additional resources is commonly *need-based*, which in many cases would be more accurately characterized as *want-based* justification. In any event, it's fair to say, need-based justifications do not go through the same rigor as value-based justifications. The latter would involve a comparison of the prospective employee's fully burdened cost to the projected value that individual is expected to bring back to the company. Hiring decisions are considered financially prudent when the projected return value exceeds the individual's fully burdened cost, and imprudent when the opposite is true. With that in mind, let's take a closer look at need-based versus value-based hiring justification.

One factor that will commonly influence the ease or difficulty of getting additional resources approved is the company's current financial condition. When business performance is good, there is typically less rigor applied to the resource hiring process. That means hiring managers have an easier time getting additional resources approved, with or without quantified value justification. Unfortunately, therein lies the problem. Why, you might be wondering? Because the lack of rigor will almost certainly result in hiring too many non-essential resources. In which case, instead of helping businesses advance, those resources often end up doing nothing more than watching over *real* work being done by others. Meaning, doing more counting, analysis, controlling, and other superfluous work. While a reasonable amount of the noted activities is essential in most businesses, too much is a waste of time and money.

Need-based hiring justification is also common when the opposite condition exists. In other words, business performance is not good. In those situations, a hiring manager might convince approving managers that additional analysis and control is precisely what the company needs to get back on track. The fact of the matter, blind faith (non-value quantified) resource approvals are risky at best. Although I must admit, I've seen blind faith hiring go both ways, meaning some proved worthwhile while others did not. I have witnessed situations in which a new hire, such as a financial analyst or controller, turn out to be exactly what was needed to bring challenging business matters under control. The added checks and balances and increased awareness and accountability did wonders to help managers make better informed decisions, which in turn helped advance the business.

I have also seen the opposite occur. Meaning, the added resources increased existing bureaucracy or performed meaningless analysis, which did nothing to help the business. My point being, you can go with blind faith hiring and hope for the best. Or, you can go with a more reliable and less risky value-based approach. As a long-standing people manager, I will tell you there is no comparison between value-based and need-based hiring decisions. Hence, my position on the matter is clear. For the most part, if you want an additional resource, you must justify it on the basis of value. I should also point out that quantifying return value goes beyond just the initial approval process. There is a certain amount of after the fact rigor that must be applied to validate a prudent value-based hiring decision was actually made. Otherwise, it may be necessary to subsequently course correct, which is never pleasant. Especially for individuals whose jobs are on the line, and secondarily for managers who are responsible for taking those actions.

Although I am an advocate of value-based hiring decisions, there are times when you will have no choice but to go with need-based (or faith-based) decisions. Nevertheless, after the fact rigor is always recommended.

At this point, I'd like to walk you through a few real-life hiring examples along with corresponding after the fact results. First, I will share two examples of faith-based hiring decisions, which one proved worthwhile and the other did not. Afterward, I will share two examples of value-based decisions, which, here again, one proved worthwhile and the other did not. Although three of the following four real-life examples occurred in a Managed Service rather than CSS business, they are all nonetheless relevant to the discussion at hand.

One of the Managed Services business units I worked signed a multi-year $100M contract with a large global company to manage and support their entire domestic print environment. The scope of the deal included several campus locations, as well as numerous single office locations across the USA. From the outset, this deal represented a losing proposition. We lost approximately $10M each of the first two years of this seven-year contract. Basically, we were dealing with a runaway situation that was screaming for attention.

After several disappointing executive management reviews, two personnel actions were ultimately taken. First, the client manager was replaced with someone who was more diplomatically forceful and capable of achieving better balance between the client and our BU. Previously, the relationship was very much one-sided, favoring the client. The second personnel action involved adding a knowledgeable and experienced finance manager to the dedicated deal management team. Previously, the deal was supported by a shared financial analyst who was responsible for supporting multiple deals, which meant this deal received minimal attention. Clearly, this was not just another standard deal. It was large and complex, which meant it had to be staffed differently in order for the deal to be successful.

Long story short, the new finance manager delved quickly and deeply into the problem areas and systematically led several successful profit improvement initiatives. After losing approximately $20M during the first two years of the deal life, the bleeding (so to speak) was essentially brought under control. Given the challenging deal solution assumptions that were made, we would never make money on this deal. However, after two disastrous years, we were able to keep the deal running at essentially break-even.

It took the right people with the necessary knowledge and skills to get this deal back on track. Replacing the client manager and, in particular, adding a dedicated finance manager worked wonders to improve the financial performance of this very challenging deal. There was no way to realistically quantify the return value of the finance manager when the resource hiring decision was being made. However, we were confident that with the right person and maniacal focus we could improve the deal financial performance. Although this was a need-based (or faith-based) hiring decision, the end result definitely proved to be worthwhile.

Incidentally, the hard lesson learned from this particularly challenging deal, investing in a logo (meaning a big-name client) can turn into a very expensive proposition. The fact of the matter, businesses that wish to grow or establish dominance, especially in a competitive environment, will often have to make risky decisions. In this case, the BU decided to invest in one of the big global players in a particular industry sector. The reasoning, if we could successfully win over one dominant player in that industry and do a good job supporting that client, other big players would likely follow. I'd like to make the following comment regarding this idealistic assumption. In business, there is a difference between making a strategic decision and an outright foolish one. In retrospect, given the obvious risk we took and the magnitude of the resulting financial loss, this decision clearly fell into the latter category.

Next, I'd like to talk about the non-worthwhile faith-based hiring decision example. But, before I do, I'd like to make a few comments. In the business world, when something isn't working as planned or anticipated, changes are sure to come. But, here's the thing about changes. Oftentimes, those changes end up being more motion than progress. How many times in your career have you seen changeover from centralized to decentralized management structure? How many times have you seen the exact opposite occur after a new executive manager comes in with his so-called *revolutionary ideas,* which end up fizzling during the implementation phase? How many times have you seen changes in regional management structure, adding or consolidating region managers to an organization? Okay, I'll stop there. My point being, these changes often end up being nothing more than costly motion. Furthermore, in many cases the changes result in unnecessary internal disruption and, even worse, upsetting and confusing customers.

Let's get back to my example. A few years ago, the BU I worked moved from a classic three region structure to five regions within the USA. At that time, revenue was running relatively flat and gross margin was slightly better than break-even, which meant something had to be done to try to improve financial performance. So, guess what happened? In an effort to improve both the top line and bottom line, BU management came up with the grandiose idea of moving from three to five regions, believing that change would somehow improve matters. In retrospect, the change ultimately accomplished nothing more than promote two people to regional manager, which of course also meant adding corresponding overhead expense. Along with the structural change, the regional account portfolios had to be changed, which meant a significant number of customer accounts had to move from one regional portfolio to another.

Incidentally, it didn't end there. In many cases, the five region managers felt compelled to personally reach out to several of their respective high profile and/or highly sensitive clients to provide them assurance they would continue to receive the personal attention they deserved. Based on after the fact results, it's safe to say, after six months of employee and account designation turmoil, there was no measurable improvement in revenue or margin. I am not suggesting organizational realignments such as the one described should never occur. Of course, as businesses grow and change, so too should organizational structures be adjusted to support those changes. But, when there is no growth occurring in the business, expecting revenue and profit to improve by simply expanding the management structure is, how shall I put this? Illusionary!

Now let's discuss the two value-based hiring decision examples, starting with the one that did not prove worthwhile. Generally speaking, as the number of contracts in a service business grows, so too does the requirement for direct labor resources. Similarly, the greater the projected sales volume, the more sales resources are usually required. Following is a common scenario that precipitates hiring additional Sales and Pursuit resources in a Managed Services business unit.

During the annual budgeting process, corporate management challenged the BU to achieve higher sales volume, to which BU management responded with a request for additional Sales and Pursuit resources that would be required to achieve the higher sales volume. One of the most common approaches used to justify additional Sales and Pursuit resources is utilizing a revenue per employee guideline. Without getting distracted by a lengthy discussion regarding typical ever-growing stretch goals, let's assume the current annual revenue per employee is $2M. In which case, if the company wants to grow revenue by $50M, they would have to add 25 Sales and Pursuit resources.

Let's assume the request for an additional 25 Sales and Pursuit resources is approved and those individuals are brought on board. Next, the new fiscal year is kicked off with a grand and costly National Sales meeting. Everyone comes out of the Sales meeting fired up and ready to tackle their aggressive sales quotas. Shortly thereafter, reality sets in.

As they approach the end of the 1st quarter, Sales signals they will not make their Q1 numbers. But, there is no need to panic. They'll make up the Q1 shortfall in the subsequent quarters. So, they add the Q1 shortfall to the Q2 – Q4 forecast, demonstrating they will still achieve the total year budget.

What do you think happens next? You guessed it! The end of Q2 is approaching, and Sales once again signals they will not make the Q2 numbers. Now they are facing a real dilemma. What should they do? Depending on the size of the shortfall and the probabilities assigned to deals in the sales funnel, they can do one of two things. Spread the Q2 shortfall into the Q3 and Q4 forecast, or concede they will not achieve the total year budget by adjusting down their total year forecast. Either way, at this point management concern is certainly elevated. If Sales goes with the spread approach, they will be given a reprieve for one additional quarter. If they go with dropping the total year forecast, they will surely face pressure to find ways to correspondingly reduce cost in order to preserve as much gross margin as reasonably possible.

In organizations like Sales and Pursuit, there is only so much cost you can squeeze out by cutting down travel, slowing down purchases, and taking other marginally effective cost cutting actions. *Real* cost reduction will only be achieved by reducing the number of people in the organization. That said, let's get back to our scenario. Q3 ends with another miss and panic sets in. The probability of achieving the total year budget is out the window. At this point, they bring in Finance and HR personnel to help determine the best way to reduce corresponding cost. In other words, work up a headcount reduction plan. If for no other reason, demonstrate the company takes commitment seriously, which will likely result in a few executive heads to roll. However, the brunt of the impact will surely be felt by the individual contributors in the Sales and Pursuit organizations. Most likely, many of the very same people that were hired less than one year ago.

I painted a rather bleak picture to make a point, which, believe it or not, is true to life in many cases. Let's consider the same scenario again. Only this time, assume the desired outcome was achieved. In other words, the total year revenue goal was attained. If that were to actually happen, it's important to be mindful that revenue growth does not occur simply because an organization added Sales and Pursuit resources. First and foremost, the company needs to possess products and/or services customers actually need and want. Furthermore, sales growth initiatives typically need to be accompanied by aggressive marketing and promotion campaigns that entice customers to buy more products and/or services. It's the combination of all three (products/services, marketing, and sales) that produce success, not just adding Sales and Pursuit personnel. By the way, you can have the biggest and the best sales force, but without compelling products or solutions, your ability to increase revenue is limited at best. Conversely, you can have the best products or solutions, but without an adequate size sales force and capable salespeople, your revenue growth will likewise be limited.

Finally, let's discuss the value-based hiring decision that proved to be worthwhile. In this case, the hiring manager justified bringing on a specialty systems analyst for a one-time need. Specifically, we were experiencing recurring performance issues with a homegrown business application system, which was written in a relatively unpopular computer language by someone who had long left the company. The system problems were causing employee productivity losses, which we estimated to be approximately $500K/year. Our choices were clear. Either live indefinitely with the inherent issues, or do something to fix the root problem. We decided on the latter course of action for obvious reasons. We brought in an external systems analyst with whom we signed a six month agreement, which contained several time-based progress milestones. The contract was an hourly fee agreement, which we estimated would end up costing approximately $200K to fix the problem. If our estimate was correct, the cost of the project represented less than half of the annual productivity loss we were experiencing.

Fast forward six months, the project was deemed a resounding success, which of course we were delighted with the outcome. Incidentally, what often happens in these situations, the hiring manager is so impressed with these so called *miracle workers,* they are reluctant to release the resource when the one-time project is completed. Instead, they attempt to justify keeping the resource on board to address other needs, which some may prove worthwhile while others will almost certainly not. In some situations, the hiring manager may even attempt to justify converting the specialty resource to a permanent employee. For the record, we did neither. We released the resource once the original project was successfully completed.

The potential danger with hiring a specialty resource like the one described, a time may soon come when it's no longer economically justifiable to keep the resource on board. When that happens, you are suddenly confronted with another issue, namely, a potential termination decision. No matter how you look at these types of situations, it always comes down to the value proposition. If there is quantifiable on-going value to be realized, that is greater than the resource cost, keeping the individual around makes sense? On the other hand, if it turns out the individual is only occasionally needed, keeping her around beyond the original engagement, or hiring her as a permanent employee is simply not smart business.

Bottom line, from a risk management standpoint, given the option of going with need-based versus quantified value-based hiring justification, the latter is almost always a safer bet. However, as pointed out in one of the examples above, utilizing value-based justification does not necessarily guarantee a favorable outcome. Incidentally, there will be situations in which quantifying projected value is simply not possible, leaving you no choice but to go with a faith-based hiring decision. In those cases, in lieu of leveraging quantitative data, applying a reasonable amount of foresight, intuition, and common sense will always serve you better than simply going with blind faith. Furthermore, a post-hiring evaluation should always be done to determine whether or not a wise hiring decision was actually made.

Chapter 10

Direct Labor Resource Cost and Value Management

Direct labor resources represent the engine that runs most businesses. Without them, products are not produced, software and solutions are not developed, and customers are not serviced and supported. Assuming resources are well placed and trained, there is typically a correlation between the number of direct labor resources and output volume. When we talk about managing the impact direct labor has on the P&L, we're really talking about ways to maximize resource utilization with such things as: standardizing, training and development, streamlining business processes, and more. In services businesses, improving utilization starts with understanding where you are today and where you want to be in the future, which makes the use of a Field Service Management System and Call Management System essential in a CSS organization. Since we talked fairly extensively about both systems in Chapter 8, I will refrain from discussing additional details.

Without the benefit of reports generated from the above two mentioned systems, there is no reasonable way of knowing whether you are under or over-utilizing direct labor resources. Moreover, if not managed properly, both under and over-utilization can be equally consequential from a cost and/or customer satisfaction standpoint. From a cost standpoint, underutilization is obviously not good for business. Overutilization can also be costly if you are incurring overtime expense to pay for that overutilization. From a customer satisfaction standpoint, customers will view underutilization as something positive because technicians are more readily available than they might otherwise be. On the other hand, customers will view overutilization as something negative because they will have to wait longer for a technician to be available.

Once you have established a utilization baseline of let's say 65% for field technicians, you can then start drilling down into the Field Service Management System report details to look for improvement opportunities. In other words, look for ways to get your field technician utilization rate closer to let's say 70%. For example, you might notice significant utilization variations amongst district offices, which may require redistribution of resources. Or you might find that a particular category of labor, let's say L3 technicians are underutilized, which may require moving some of those highly skilled resources elsewhere within the organization where they can be better utilized. When analyzing these reports, it's important to distinguish anomalies from persistent problems. Occasional under or overutilization is normal. However, constant under or overutilization is almost guaranteed to have adverse ramifications. The same is true for customer service and technical support agent utilization, as depicted in Call Management System reports. The only difference, the utilization rates for those reps are likely higher, maybe 85% actual rate and 90% targeted improvement rate.

In service businesses, it's very common to categorize direct labor resources as being either dedicated or shared. Dedicated resources are tied to a particular contracted deal or customer that is typically assigned a unique cost center number for accounting and P&L reporting purposes. In those cases, all of the direct labor cost is captured in the customer designated cost center and subsequently reflected in the corresponding Deal or Customer P&L.

Accounting for labor cost doesn't get any easier and more straightforward. On the other hand, accounting for shared resource cost is more involved. Meaning, there are two steps required to get cost assigned to the ultimately intended cost center. The initial cost capture is straightforward. That is to say, all of the labor related cost for those resources is initially posted to the shared cost center those individuals are assigned. The second step involves moving reported labor cost from the shared cost center to the ultimately intended cost center, whether that be for a particular contracted deal, customer, or else. That is where automated cost posting functionality, which are built into robust Field Service Management systems, is invaluable. Next, we will talk about the impact standardization has on resource utilization, followed by the impact from training and development, and lastly the impact from streamlining business processes.

Standardization

In virtually all businesses, including both product and service businesses, standardization is a powerful means of maximizing resource utilization. Generally speaking, the more a company standardizes, the lower will be the cost of manufacturing products or delivering services, which ultimately results in better ability to compete. If your competitors are leveraging standardized methods and processes and your company is not, it's virtually impossible for your company to compete on the basis of cost and price. Let's face it, in the marketplace price is king, which is especially true as products and service become increasingly commoditized.

As with most personal decisions one contemplates, business decisions must consider all of the related pros and cons before a final decision is made. Making standardization decisions in service businesses are no different. One of the pros that will likely be given maximum consideration is lowering operating cost. However, the flip side of lowering operating cost is potentially adversely impacting customer satisfaction. Service organizations must always be mindful of the impact standardization might have on their clients. The obvious reason, some customers may not be happy with how they are affected by standardization. Therefore, some extra effort may be required to smooth things over with some clients beforehand, *not* after you have already implemented standardized processes.

For example, a CSS organization might decide to reorganize Technical Support from a client specific support structure to a centralized structure that handles all clients. From a call management standpoint, a centralized structure would almost certainly be more efficient and better suited to handle call volume fluctuations, in particular call spikes. Although that may be beneficial for the CSS organization from a process efficiency and cost effectiveness standpoint, customers may not like the impact the change has on them. The reason being, they may have grown accustomed and comfortable talking with a handful of client dedicated technicians, and had a sense those technicians understood their unique business needs. Being funneled into a general pool of technical support technicians will certainly not give them the same sense of being a *special client*.

Obviously, this type of change can backfire on the CSS organization if not handled with extraordinary care. In particular, establishing a reasonable level of comfort with affected clients beforehand. It may even require some sort of compromise, or a good faith reciprocity gesture on the part of CSS. The example I just shared represents only one of numerous potential impacts that could result from standardization. I simply wanted to convey that there are a multitude of factors that have to be considered when making a standardization decision. The obvious reason, it's not just the impact on the company's business processes and financial performance that matter. More importantly is the impact on the client and their willingness to accept the standardization change.

Let's look at an example where standardized processes already exist; however, a new contract that was just signed by a big corporate client contains non-standard service and support requirements. Speaking from personal experience, I can tell you this is something that is not unusual. At any rate, let's assume you have a team of 500 delivery personnel who are responsible for supporting the entire installed customer base. And, to a large extent, your team leverages standardized processes. Wouldn't it be nice if it remained that way? Sure it would, but here's the thing. When new deals are being sold, in particular to big corporate clients, those clients will often request non-standard deliverables, which your delivery organization cannot accommodate without making process changes. As challenging as that may be for the delivery organization, the sales organization is generally only interested in one thing, selling the deal (deliverable or not).

Although delivery personnel are often involved in the deal solution process, any push-back on their part is usually met with considerable pressure to back off and allow the deal to move forward as requested by the client. It's not hard to guess what happens next. The deal is signed and the non-standard deliverables evolve from being a contract negotiation challenge for the sales team to a long-term deliverables challenge for the delivery team. As difficult as it may be, the delivery organization will eventually find ways to make the one-off deliverables work, which could take several months to implement and stabilize. Unfortunately, lurking behind one deliverable challenge will typically be another one-off challenge the delivery organization will soon be facing. Bottom line, it's the delivery organization that is typically left holding the bag (so to speak) in these situations.

By the way, if the delivery organization cannot figure out how to address the one-off challenges, they will be viewed as the *bad guys*. Meanwhile, the sales team members get to walk away with their incentive compensation check after the deal is signed. It goes without saying, there are times when customers can be unreasonably demanding. However, it's amazing how flexible many of those customers become when you make it interesting for them with, let's say, a lower price. The point being, standardization is clearly a good thing from a resource utilization standpoint. And, as long as the sales team is willing to work with clients to keep deliverables as standard as possible, it can be a win/win/win solution. Meaning, it can help the delivery organization lower cost, provide the customer a more competitive price, and the sales team still get their incentive compensation, only not at the cost of making it more difficult for the delivery organization.

I would like to make one final point regarding additional benefits derived from standardizing service delivery. Standardized delivery models inherently offer more opportunity to segment and potentially move portions of the support to lower cost locations. And yes, that may mean offshoring some of the work. Lower cost can also mean moving some work to a less costly part of the nation. By the way, my comment regarding offshoring should not be construed as a blind endorsement for offshoring work because it's not. I will tell you from personal experience, effective offshoring does not come easy and it does not always work as intended. Typically, there are several challenges that have to be overcome implementing a successful offshore solution. Nevertheless, sometimes you simply have no choice but to go that route. The primary reason, if your competitors are taking advantage of low-cost offshore support and you are not, your ability to compete will almost certainly be more challenging.

Training and Development

Another thing that can improve direct labor resource utilization is training initiatives. Although typically done with the best intentions, training initiatives often turn out to be ineffective. Why you might ask? Because how training is created and delivered matters as much as the content itself. First and foremost, failed initiatives often lack involvement by people from the organization being trained. Generally speaking, trainees are more likely to embrace training that is created and delivered by someone within their own organization. Whereas, training that is created and delivered by *outsiders* is almost never received with the same level of interest and enthusiasm. Throughout my career I have participated in the development and rollout of several training initiatives. By far, initiatives that involved people from the organization being trained proved more effective and successful.

Allow me to share an example of a recent personal experience. We assembled a team to develop and deliver P&L improvement training to a national team of Account Delivery Mangers (ADMs). The training involved two separate segments. The first segment covered a basic understanding of P&L management, which was delivered by a credible and well-respected finance manager. This individual was able to take a relatively complicated subject and break it down to simple, straightforward language, while utilizing several examples to help solidify trainee understanding. The feedback we received from this segment of the training was overwhelmingly positive.

The second segment, which was delivered by an individual from the delivery management community, focused on how to effectively leverage available levers and knobs to improve contracted deal profitability. From past failed experience, we thought it would be best to have the training delivered by someone within the trainee community, instead of an outsider such as a finance or business analyst. Just as with the first training segment, success versus failure came down to one word, credibility. In the latter case, who more credible than someone who has lived the experience to talk about how to successfully leverage available levers and knobs? If the same exact training material had been delivered by a finance or business analyst, I can almost guarantee we would not have achieved the same positive results. Why? Because, as most of us know from our own experiences, the person telling the story (delivering the training) matters as much as the story itself (the training material).

In addition to who and how training is most effectively delivered, there are a few training best practices I would like to discuss, starting with the importance of pre-requisite foundational knowledge. You can have the best training material possible and still fail miserably with your rollout. One of the principal reasons, the people you are training do not possess sufficient pre-requisite foundational knowledge. For example, you cannot effectively deliver P&L management training to a group of people who do not at least possess fundamental financial knowledge. Just as you cannot effectively deliver technical training to a group of people who do not possess fundamental product knowledge.

Throughout my career, I've seen this simple-minded approach attempted and fail several times. We're not talking about the trainees' intellectual capacity here. Instead, we're talking about the fact that most training is progressive and works like building blocks, with one layer added on top of another. My point being, when you launch a training initiative, make sure the training will be delivered to people who possess the necessary foundational knowledge. Otherwise, the rollout of your training initiative is almost guaranteed to fail.

Next, I'd like to talk about two important aspects of training that could very well make the difference between success and failure. The first is regarding delivery method, and the second is regarding the training audience size and make-up. I'd like to start by stating, dialog will always produce better results than monolog. Regardless of who you place in front of the trainees, if that person is robotically walking through a PowerPoint presentation, the training will most likely result in failure. On the other hand, utilizing a trainer that can effectively engage the audience and encourage dialog amongst the trainees will most likely result in success. No one likes to be talked to. If you want people to really listen and learn, you must find a way to engage them in the conversation.

In order to start the conversation, the trainer must first find a way to break the ice with the trainees. So, what's the best way to do that? Know your audience. Encourage one or more people in the audience who you know to get the conversation started with questions or comments. It never ceases to amaze me, when one individual starts, others will invariably follow. And before you know it, you have much of the training audience contributing to a robust training event. What better way to get the juices flowing? Dialog is contagious! Getting started is the only hard part. So, when you're deciding on the best person to deliver the training, don't make the common mistake of selecting the person who possesses the most subject matter knowledge. If that person cannot relate to the trainees, and is unable to get them involved in a conversation, you chose the wrong person. Instead, settle for someone with less knowledge if you have to, as long as she possesses the necessary people skills to make the training experience engaging and successful.

Now let's move on to the importance of training audience size and make-up. Typically, there are several factors that go into training decisions, which some will be influenced by economic considerations. Audience size is clearly one factor that has economic implications. I believe it's fair to say, the smaller the training audience, generally the better the training results. For example, it would be difficult for anyone to argue that 1:1 training produces the best results. The reason being, the trainer who is conveying the knowledge can instantly see whether or not the information is acknowledged and understood by the trainee. In which case, if deemed necessary, the trainer can quickly react with changes to the delivery approach. But, here is the problem with 1:1 training. It's very expensive!

The next best thing from both an economic and results standpoint is small group training of, let's say, 1 trainer to roughly 10 trainees. Although there are limited places for trainees to hide in these situations, there is no guarantee the training material will be absorbed by everyone. On the other hand, small group training is not nearly as expensive as 1:1 training. Next, let's assume a group of 50 individuals are being trained. Undoubtedly, from a cost perspective, that would be the most economical approach. However, it's virtually guaranteed some trainees will walk out of the training session with little or no more knowledge than when they walked into the training.

Like most business decisions, optimal training group size comes down to tradeoff value. For example, if you're doing general product knowledge training for a team of salespeople, a 1 to 50 approach may be perfectly acceptable. After all, salespeople are typically not expected to be product knowledge specialists. So, if they miss some of the training points, no big deal. On the other hand, if you're training 50 technicians on knowledge they will require to service and support new product, it is a big deal if some of those technicians walk out of the training clueless. In that case, a 1 to 10 training approach might be more suitable. Bottom line, training group size matters from both an affectivity and economic standpoint. Furthermore, a well-trained workforce, particularly in service businesses, is one of the principal keys to success.

The make-up of a training audience is also important. Unlike a classic academic environment, whereby diversity typically enhances the educational experience, the opposite is generally true in a corporate training environment. A good example of the former is a classroom of experienced professionals participating in an MBA program. The diversity and real-life experiences each student brings to the class and shares with classmates will undoubtedly enrich the educational experience. On the other hand, I found homogeneity to be more important than diversity in a corporate training environment. The reason being, like professionals typically relate better and are more comfortable with one another. Furthermore, people in large mixed training audiences are often reluctant to ask questions or make comments, fearing they may sound stupid. Whereas, those same fears/concerns are generally not nearly as evident when like professionals are being trained. Incidentally, if you want to see trainees at their best, have their manager participate in the training session. It's amazing how much more attentive and alive people tend to be when the person responsible for their performance review is in the same room.

At this point, I'd like to share a related personal experience. One of the most successful training series I ever participated was delivering operations and finance management training to several individual teams of ADMs. Members of each team reported to 1 of 5 regional portfolio managers. Furthermore, the individuals on each team were very comfortable with one another since they regularly met to discuss routine business matters with their manager. Moreover, they all had common problems and challenges. So, they naturally related well to one another. The great thing about these training events, one individual would ask a question or make a comment, which would quickly be followed by another person engaging in the conversation. The best way to describe what occurred, it was contagious in a good way. The resulting dialog was encouraging, and the training experience was successful. I am confident, if you were to ask the individual participants about both the experience and the outcome, the overwhelming majority would agree with my assessment.

For economic or other business reasons, let's assume you have no choice but to deliver training to a large group of diversified professionals who routinely work with one another. This is precisely what happened at a recent National Sales and Services Kick-off Meeting training event. If you're not familiar with these annual kick-off meetings, I will tell you they are very expensive. And, they take numerous people away from their day-to-day job responsibilities for the better part of a week. Thus, management will do everything reasonably possible to make the best use of allotted time, including having larger than ideal focused training sessions.

In the focused training session I am about to describe, there were approximately 75 ADMs plus 25 people from various support functions like Finance and Business Operations. The subject matter was best practices Deal P&L management, which we were allotted three hours for the training event. I realize that sounds like a lot of time for a breakout training event. Given the broad and complex subject matter, that was the minimum amount of time we required. So, here is what we did to make the best use of the allotted time. Before starting the training session, we told the trainees that at the end of the presentation segment we would assemble breakout teams to work through a related business scenario. That pre-training announcement encouraged most attendees to pay closer attention than they might otherwise have. It worked much like your teacher in high school or professor in college saying "pay special attention to the following because it will be on the test." In our situation, I am quite sure the motivating factor was, no one wanted to appear clueless in front of their peers during the breakout session.

As promised, when the presentation segment was completed, we assembled ten breakout teams with approximately ten people on each team. We provided each team the same written business scenario along with additional complementary material, and informed them they had one hour to solve the problem. Also, we told them each team had to select a spokesperson who would be given ten minutes to present the team's findings. The interactions that occurred during the group breakouts were lively and interesting. Furthermore, the discussion that occurred when the team findings were presented to the entire training audience was a magnificent thing to watch. Best of all, it was remarkable to see the whole room come alive with constructive and healthy dialog. In retrospect, I'd have to say this training event proved to be as close to ideal as possible. By the way, after the participants completed the feedback evaluation for the entire kick-off meeting, this event received the best overall breakout training rating. The lesson learned, with a little ingenuity and foresight, you can turn a challenging situation like this large mixed group training event into successful outcome.

Although it may not be obvious to everyone, mentoring is an ideal complement to professional training and development. I will explain the reason in a moment. Most professional organizations consist of individuals that possess varying levels of knowledge and experience, ranging from novice to expert level. Furthermore, it's important to be mindful, training is typically not a one-time event. In any event, training alone can only go so far to help produce valuable and knowledgeable resources. It must be coupled with experience, which can come from a couple of different sources, one's own experience and/or mentor shared experience. Regarding the latter, assigning an expert level mentor to guide and assist a novice professional can both enhance and expedite the learning and development process.

Alternatively, it's certainly possible for individuals to strictly learn from their own experiences, but that approach will definitely be a slower and longer path to follow. Progressive training coupled with mentoring is unquestionably the shorter and more expeditious path. Sure, mentoring can take some otherwise productive time away from the expert level resource. However, in most cases, the payback to the organization makes mentoring a worthwhile investment.

Finally, I'd like to add, as important as training and development is to success, one must be mindful of its limitations. Let me give you a vivid example of what I am referring. I was personally involved in a long-term training initiative to convert approximately 100 ADMs to P&L managers. As subtle as that may sound, it wasn't. There is a huge difference between simply managing a customer account and being held accountable for profit contribution. Most of the people I am referring were initially hired as operations managers, meaning they were responsible for delivering contracted services and achieving stated levels of customer satisfaction. However, they were not held accountable for the P&L performance of their respective contracted deal. It's important to point out that several of these individuals possessed absolutely no prior P&L management experience. The fact of the matter, they did not have to because that was not part of the original job requirement. Therein lies the biggest challenge we faced, which I will explain in a moment.

Although the organization previously produced Deal P&Ls, they were virtually useless. The reason being, those P&Ls were generated by a small team of offshore financial resources that were inexperienced and were not properly trained. Bottom line, there were several significant cost omissions in the P&Ls, which created the illusion that most of the deals were very profitable. Once we straightened out the accounting issues and started producing accurate and reliable Deal P&Ls, management suddenly realized several of our contracted deals were actually in financial trouble. Shortly thereafter, the ADM training initiative I referred to earlier was launched. Incidentally, the previous P&Ls were so outrageously misstated that if a deal did not reflect 50% or greater gross margin it was considered a loser. The fact of the matter, not only were essentially all of the deals not producing anywhere near 50% gross margin, several were actually under water. In other words, generating negative gross margin.

Let's get back to the P&L management training initiative. After more than one year of progressive P&L training, we failed to realize the lofty goal we set for ourselves, namely, converting 100% of the operations managers to P&L managers. To be clear, this was sporadic training that occurred throughout the year, which was equivalent to approximately four weeks of training. In the final analysis, we actually realized approximately 75% of our goal. In which case, 25% of the ADMs proved to be proficient at managing Deal P&Ls, and another 50% absorbed sufficient knowledge to adequately manage P&Ls. The remaining 25% were still in various stages of cluelessness regarding P&L management. Why you might be wondering? Some people, as good as they were operations managers, were unable to make the connection between business activities and the financials. Simply put, grasping financial concepts was simply not in their DNA, which meant there was no way we would achieve 100% of our goal, even with additional training.

Instead, we were faced with the hard reality that several of those ADMs needed to be replaced with people who possessed the newly required skills. I realize it's not fair that someone would be displaced for an after the fact job requirement. Welcome to the ever-challenging and sometimes very unfair world of business! The lesson learned, you can invest all you want in training and development, but in some cases, it will simply not produce desired results. The reason being, if the people you are training do not possess the aptitude, desire, and/or willingness to learn because they are suddenly out of their comfort zone, you are basically wasting time and money training those individuals.

Streamlining Business Processes

Finally, let's talk about maximizing direct labor resource utilization by streamlining and/or improving business processes. Once you have honed in on a problematic and/or antiquated business process, the first thing you need to do is flowchart the existing process. If a flowchart already exists, make sure it's accurate and up to date. If a flowchart does not exist, create one. In either case, be sure to involve subject matter experts in this important first step, as well as all of the subsequent process rebuilding steps.

Some companies do a good job keeping their business processes up to date. Other companies do the complete opposite, from having no documentation to having neglected or outdated process documentation. When one of the latter conditions exists, business processes are only as good as the quality and accuracy of verbal information that is passed down from one employee to the next, which is really a dangerous way to run a business. That is particularly true in situations there is significant employee attrition. Even worse, are situations in which a key employee, who mentally possesses undocumented business processes, never shows up for work again for whatever reason. If and when that happens, you will undoubtedly experience unpleasant consequences, as well as have a significant time consuming challenge on your hands. Meaning, you will have to document those processes starting with a blank sheet of paper.

For the most part, business processes become outdated or obsolete when one of the following events occurs: introduction of a new business system or tool, acquisition, divestiture, and any number of other significant changes that may occur in a company. As these fast-moving and challenging activities occur, one of the last things busy people think about is updating business process documents. That is, until they are faced with the consequences of having outdated documentation. Ideally, organizations should routinely review their business process documents, and update them whenever a significant change occurs in the business. There are no such things as everlasting business processes. As changes occur in a business, so too must those changes be reflected in updated process documents. The reason being, how business gets done will often influence resource utilization, which will ultimately influence business profitability.

Chapter 11

Indirect Labor Resource Cost and Value Management

I'd like to start this chapter by stating the obvious. Most companies cannot successfully operate without a reasonable number of indirect or overhead resources. That said, the fundamental challenge companies face is ensuring the return value of indirect labor resources outweigh their cost. Just as with direct labor, obtaining indirect labor cost is relatively straightforward. It's simply a matter of capturing salary plus fringe and all other employee-related expenses for those individuals. However, capturing indirect labor value is considerably more difficult and less precise than capturing direct labor value. The primary reason, there is less correlation between indirect resources and business volume as there is with direct resources. Therefore, determining the value of indirect resources must oftentimes be based on either reported changes in related performance indicators or reasonable correlating assumptions.

Let's briefly consider one category of overhead resources, namely, management. Unless you're running a small mom and pop operation, most companies require a reasonable amount of management leadership. Without management, companies would lack the vision and direction required to successfully run the business. Furthermore, as companies grow in size and complexity, they normally require specialty resources in the following overhead functions. Finance to manage the accounting and financial analysis. Human Resources to manage the workforce. Legal to provide legal protection and risk management. And, any number of other administrative and support functions required to effectively run the business. Therefore, the question regarding overhead resources is not whether they are required or not. It's a question of how many are truly necessary and justifiable on the basis of cost versus return value. Unfortunately, many companies do not make indirect resource hiring decisions with payback value in mind. That is one of the primary reasons so many companies end up with too many indirect resources, which, in many cases, do nothing more than burden the business with unnecessary cost.

Indirect Resources Have Varying Impact on Profitability

Indirect resources tend to either be project oriented or part of general overhead. Although a reasonable number of general overhead resources are essential to run most businesses, overhead functions are often overstaffed. In which case, the value of some of those resources is questionable at best. On the other hand, the value of project oriented indirect resources is more easily identified and, in most cases, worthwhile with the following condition. Those resources must be released or re-assigned when the project they are hired to do is completed. Keeping them around to handle non-critical projects, or just in case they may be needed in the future, is simply not smart business.

At this point, I'd like to share a couple of real-life examples of newly assigned indirect resources, which one proved worthwhile and the other did not. The worthwhile example involved moving an existing indirect resource into a newly created long-term project. This particular individual was sought after because he possessed extensive business knowledge and experience, as well as extraordinary data mining skills, which both were required to successfully tackle this project. Actually, this individual was relentless when it came to data mining. Anecdotally, we referred to him as the data maniac. The project he was tasked involved a runaway problem with embedded lease write-offs, which amounted to $3-4M per year. If you're familiar with embedded leases that are associated with contracted services, great! If you're not, it's not terribly important to the underlining point I am trying to make. Suffice to say, this problem was absolutely eating away at what could have otherwise been profit for this relatively new business unit, which incidentally had not yet contributed any profit to the business.

It took several months of concentrated effort from this particular individual, plus lots of support from a cross-functional team to achieve initial success, which meant stopping the problem from growing further. After several more months of collaborative effort, we started to see a reversal in the trend. In other words, old long-standing issues were rapidly being resolved. Fast forwarding a couple years, the ongoing monthly embedded lease variance was essentially brought down to zero, and remained at roughly zero for several years that followed. To say the least, this was a remarkable accomplishment, which saved the company tens of millions of dollars. It was done with the right expert resource leading the effort, along with a great deal of support and perseverance from a cross-functional team that systematically chipped away at old lingering problems. Furthermore, outdated business processes, which were contributing to the problem, were updated to prevent similar issues from occurring in the future.

With regard to return value, there was no clear and concise way of establishing the actual value this particular individual brought back to the organization. Although, we do know losses were running at $3-4M per year before the problem was confronted head on. If we take a very conservative approach and consider just two years savings, we avoided $6-8M embedded lease write-offs. Comparing that to this individual's fully burdened cost, plus the cost of ½ dozen or so part-time resources who assisted with the project during the two years, brings the total cost to less than $1M. Therefore, conservatively speaking, this project saved the company a minimum of $5M after expenses. Not bad, when you consider the fact this one indirect resource was principally responsible for this incredible turnaround.

Along these lines, I'd like to make one additional comment regarding new BUs. Generally speaking, the focus of a new BU is more on marketing and growing the business, and less on business controls and processes. That is precisely the reason focused sweeps like the one just described are particularly important for the long-term vitality and profitability of the new BU. Of course, focused sweeps are also useful in well-established businesses. The difference being, in well-established businesses, you generally have to look harder and deeper to find significant profit improvement opportunities. The reason being, the low hanging fruit (so to speak) will have likely already been picked.

The non-worthwhile example involved moving an existing people manager into a newly created individual contributor role, reporting to the same senior manager he reported to previously. The need for this position was the result of a recent Service organization realignment, which closely mirrored the reorganized Sales organization. Fundamentally, the move made sense since the two organizations worked very closely together and typically shared the same regional customers. The former manager I am referring volunteered for the individual contributor position principally because he had grown tired of dealing with people management issues, and particularly tired dealing with demanding and unreasonable clients. Dealing with seemingly never-ending people management issues and challenging clients can certainly contribute to management fatigue. Most ambitious individual contributors work hard to become people managers or client managers. Therefore, it's difficult for most people to understand and appreciate why someone would want to move backward into an individual contributor role. Believe me, it happens! Furthermore, when management fatigue sets in, affected managers want nothing more than to move out of their existing role, the sooner the better.

The fact of the matter, managing challenging organizations and/or clients can eventually take the wind out of your sails (so to speak). I've seen that very thing happen to several good managers who simply couldn't take it anymore. They desperately needed to get back to a more suitable situation in which they only needed to be concerned with self-management. Anyway, this particular individual ended up in a role coordinating a fairly significant regional realignment of customer accounts and widespread manager reporting changes. Without question, this was a critical one-time project that took approximately six months to complete. At that point, instead of moving this individual to an equally critical role, his manager kept him in that staff position to handle routine operations management matters. We already had a Business Operations organization in the BU that handled routine administrative matters. Therefore, there was no need for the costly redundancy.

Once again, we come back to the cost versus value principle. The cost of keeping this individual in that role beyond the initial six month project was surely greater than the incremental value he subsequently brought back to the BU. How do I know that? I witnessed it with my own eyes. The tasks this individual worked on after the initial six-month project was completed could have easily and effectively been handled by a less experienced person on the Business Operations team. By the way, I am not suggesting that a proven employee with a good track record, such as this particular individual, should simply be discarded from the company when there is no apparent immediate need for his services. However, I am suggesting management needs to do a better job assigning these individuals where they are truly needed to make meaningful contributions, even if that means having to move the person around a few times before he finally settles into a worthwhile permanent position. Sure, it's a little more work on the manager's part. But in the long run, both the employee and the company will benefit from the manager's extra effort. Besides, it's the right thing to do.

From a profit contribution standpoint, the first example I shared represents more so the exception than the rule. Realistically speaking, I'd have to say most indirect resources have limited impact on profitability. In fact, if you believe the aggregate gazillion dollars saved by indirect resources, as reflected in their resumes, it would certainly add up to be more than enough money needed to cure world hunger (sarcasm). The fact of the matter, there is a significant amount of double counting and miscounting reflected in those grossly exaggerated claims. So, what's real? In most cases, it's hard to pinpoint. But one thing is for sure, it's nowhere near the exaggerated claims commonly made by indirect resources.

Indirect Resources Tend to Creep Up in Organizations

If not watched and managed carefully, indirect resources tend to creep up in organizations beyond levels truly needed and justifiable. There is always a so-called *good reason* for adding another indirect resource to count, control, or analyze business activity. And, before you know it, you have a lopsided situation;

whereby indirect labor cost represents an ever-growing percentage of total labor cost. Although that situation should not be allowed to occur, those of us who have been in business for any length of time have witnessed otherwise. Nevertheless, when it's obvious an imbalance exists, management should take corrective action. Remember, cost is cost no matter where it occurs. Furthermore, viable companies can only carry so much indirect labor cost before it starts to negatively impact profitability and their ability to compete.

Allow me to share a real-life example of indirect resource creep, which has to do with extraordinary Finance resource growth in a BU I recently worked. When I joined the BU, it had only existed for a couple of years and was generating approximately $50M in annual revenue. Relative to the entire company size, this was a small and insignificant business unit, which senior management was apparently convinced would eventually turn into a worthwhile investment. Just as with most new BUs, we were given some leeway and allowed to operate below break-even during the first few years. At that time there was one full-time USA based financial analyst assigned to support this business, supplemented by 4-5 relatively inexperienced remote analysts located in India.

Having worked directly with each of the remote analysts, I quickly realized they were financially book smart, but clearly lacked business knowledge and experience. In which case, their usefulness was limited through no fault of their own. Having been a financial analyst myself for several years, I can tell you that without an understanding of the business you are supporting, your usefulness will be limited at best. In retrospect, the India based resources should have been better trained regarding the intricacies of the business they were supporting.

Ultimately, we did resolve this issue, but not without classic overreaction that typically occurs in business when problems like this arise. Meaning, we added a bunch of Finance resources to support the BU. Although the business grew from $50M to $250M annual revenue within a few short years, I can safely say, we added far too many permanent Finance resources. Clearly some additional resources were needed, but we definitely went overboard. Simultaneously, we moved the offshore support from India to Mexico. However, this time we did a much better job of providing the Mexico based financial analysts the necessary business and financial training. Without question, much of what we did was justified, and ultimately proved successful. However, it was definitely overkill. Meaning, we would likely have done equally well by only adding about half of those resources. Bottom line, whenever you end up in a situation in which checkers are checking the checkers and people bumping into each other (figuratively speaking), you clearly have an over-abundant resource issue that must be addressed and rectified.

Chapter 12

Internal versus External Resources

CSS organizations often utilize external resources to either augment their internal capabilities or in lieu of internal resources. The focus of this chapter is on when it makes more sense to use external versus internal resources. In this context, external resources refer to anyone other than employees. Therefore, consultants, temporary workers, as well as work that is outsourced to any number of specialty companies are all considered use of external resources. There are several cost factors that are often overlooked when managers consider using external resources. From what I have observed, the three most significant factors include: training, attrition, and management oversight cost. In order to create a true *apples to apples* comparison of external versus internal resource cost, over and above the amount actually paid external resource vendors, consideration must minimally be given to these three factors. On the other hand, fringe plus all other employee-related overhead cost must be added to the internal resource gross salary to reflect the fully burdened employee cost, which typically runs at roughly 150% of gross salary.

Now let's discuss in more detail the three above mentioned commonly overlooked external versus internal cost factors, starting with management oversight. It's important to acknowledge the fact, there is a certain amount of management oversight required by the client (in this case CSS) whenever utilizing external resources. Depending on the business arrangement between the client and vendor, there are various management oversight methods that can be utilized. One common method is an on-going review of performance reports.

In this case, if something looks odd or questionable in those reports, the client will meet with the vendor to discuss and resolve the odd/questionable issue(s). Other more formal client/vendor review methods are commonly referred to as Monthly Business Reviews (MBRs) or Quarterly Business Reviews (QBRs). In those cases, if there were few issues or problems that occurred during the review period, the time invested by the client will be limited. On the other hand, if there were significant issues/problems, the time invested by the client will be greater, resulting in higher management oversight cost. The fact of the matter, most outsourced work does not run perfectly smooth, deeming management oversight a critical component of all client/vendor business arrangements.

Next, let's talk about training cost that is associated with utilizing external resources. Responsibility for training external resources can vary along a full spectrum, from essentially being 100% client to 100% vendor responsibility. Nonetheless, the client will almost always have some level of involvement, and in some cases incur substantial training cost. The most costly scenario for the client is when they are responsible for both creating and delivering all external resource training. A less costly scenario is when *train the trainer* approach is utilized. In which case, the client is only responsible for the initial training, while the vendor is responsible for all subsequent training. The least costly scenario for the client is when they are only responsible for creating the training material, and the vendor assumes full responsibility for delivering the training. Regardless of what approach is used, external training cost is clearly something that must be considered when contemplating use of external resources.

Finally, let's talk about attrition cost related to use of external resources. Attrition rates can be especially significant in parts of the world where sought-after low-cost resources are available such as India, China, Eastern Europe, and Central and South America. The reason being, many of those sought-after resources will typically move from one company to another for even the slightest wage increase, which is totally understandable considering the typical standard of living in many of those nations. Nevertheless, as resource movement increases, so too does attrition cost, primarily due to extraordinary training and ramp-up cost. Think about the cost difference of having, let's say, 5% versus 30% annual attrition. It's important to be mindful, every time a new resource is brought into an organization, no matter how knowledgeable he may be, there will always be some training and ramp-up cost involved. So, if you are having to train 1 in 20 (5%) versus 1 in 3 (33%) external resources annually, training cost will be considerably different in those two extremes. Incidentally, for CSS organizations, I'd say the most common use of offshore resources if for Customer Service and Technical Support functions.

When External Resources Make More Economic Sense

Regarding the fundamental question, when is it better to use external versus internal resources? The answer is, it depends on the company's tolerance for risk and willingness to deal with the usual challenges associated with pursuing a more cost competitive strategy. Let's start with risk, which is always a balancing act between rewards and consequences. Rewards are usually measured in terms of dollars, and consequences in terms of impact on customer satisfaction. It goes without saying, if you could take a risk lowering labor cost and not suffer corresponding customer satisfaction consequences, who wouldn't take that risk? Unfortunately, the reality of risk-taking is never knowing the outcome beforehand.

So, if you're planning to set up new externally supported activities or migrate existing internal activities to external resources, the best advice I can give is to be analytical and methodical with your approach. Start slow and constantly evaluate and tweak as necessary, while working toward completing the changeover. Going blindly and quickly can prove to be a costly mistake. Incidentally, there are a number of reasons that can motivate companies to utilize external resources. One of the most popular reasons is desire to maximize profitability. Another popular reason is having to follow your competition to remain in the game (so to speak). The latter is not necessarily what one might consider a desirable reason, but intense competition can sometimes leave you with limited choices.

With regard to CSS businesses, besides potentially outsourcing Customer Service and Technical support, I'd say the other most commonly outsourced function is on-site service, which a third-party vendor either partially or totally takes over on-site service responsibility. In addition, the business may outsource mundane work, which is currently being done by highly skilled, highly paid resources, as well as outsource some back-office work. Since we previously discussed some of the merits and risks associated with outsourcing customer service, technical support, and on-site service, let's briefly talk about the other two above- mentioned categories, namely, mundane work and back-office work.

With virtually no exceptions, all professional employees have to deal with a certain amount of mundane work, some more than others. In some cases, highly paid professionals regularly consume a significant portion of their workday on administrative tasks that could surely be done more cost effectively elsewhere. With enough complaints from these workers, executive managers will sometimes come to their rescue.

When that happens, the first step usually taken is to create a list of the day-to-day activities that group of individuals performs, along with the average amount of time each activity typically consumes. The next step is to separate *must keep* from *mundane* activities that can potentially be offloaded. Following those two steps, there is usually a lively management team discussion regarding the merits and risks of offloading each of the mundane activities, with particular emphases on those that may negatively impact customer satisfaction. Once there is final agreement, a project plan is created listing all the activities that are to be offloaded in priority order. Normally, it's the so-called *low hanging fruit,* or activities that are expected to produce the biggest bang for the buck, that make it to the top of the list and are offloaded accordingly.

And finally, let's talk about offloading back-office work, which typically represents the least amount of risk. Examples of back-office work in a CSS organization would include such things as contract admin and billing and other relatively straightforward administrative functions that require little training to successfully perform elsewhere. That is particularly important if the functions are being moved to developing countries where attrition is expected to be extraordinarily high. Offloading back-office work is usually handled one of two ways. The first, enter into a contractual agreement with a low-cost service provider who will do the work from a near-shore or offshore location. The second, keep the work internally, but move it to a newly created Center of Excellence located in a near-shore or offshore location. Ultimately, what matters most, which option is more cost-effective and represents the lowest amount of risk. Bottom line, whether the work is done by a vendor or internal Center of Excellence, offloading back-office work can prove to be an effective cost reduction strategy.

Let's face it, virtually anything that's done internally by employees can also be done externally by consultants or contractors. Therefore, a decision to offload work to external resources usually comes down to where the work can be done better, faster, cheaper, while maintained desired quality, security, and customer satisfaction levels. Incidentally, decisions to offload work can be complicated and oftentimes emotionally charged. Some of the contributing factors might include: managers attempting to protect their employees, local or national politics, pressure from special interest groups, etc. Furthermore, it's important to point out that emotion and resistance run hottest when a company is considering sending the work outside national borders. On the other hand, there is generally more tolerance and less resistance when the work is being offloaded to low-cost areas within national borders. Whether that is due to nationalism or else, decision makers should anticipate encountering some resistance whenever contemplating moving work offshore.

From what I have observed, the attitude and willingness to utilize external resources has changed dramatically over the past several years, principally due to competitive cost pressures. More and more companies are looking externally for low-cost resource solutions just to remain competitive. Of course, there are other companies that address competitive challenges with advanced technology and automation. However, in service businesses, there is generally a limit to how far advanced technology and automation will take you. The fact of the matter, service businesses are essentially people cost businesses. In which case, if those companies want to materially impact cost, they have to continuously address the following fundamental question. How and where can work be done cheaper, better, faster? Oftentimes, that means having to leverage lower cost external resources.

Apples to Apples Internal vs. External Cost Comparison

Whenever you are doing an internal versus external resource cost comparison, your internal cost must take into account all employee-related expenses, including fringe and all other employee overhead. As previously mentioned, fully burdened employee cost typically runs at roughly 150% of gross salary. Similarly, external resource cost must consider factors beyond just what you pay your resource vendor. Depending on where the external resources are actually located, you may incur physical accommodation costs for such things as: office space, phone, network, etc. You will also incur management oversight cost, which we discussed the details earlier. The point being, for a realistic *apples to apples* cost comparison, all applicable internal and external resource related cost must be taken into account.

Depending on the type of agreement the CSS organization has with the resource vendor, they will likely pay the vendor based on one of the following methods: 1) hours worked; 2) number of incidents or events; 3) completed repairs; 4) dedicated individual(s); or 5) contracted project. These five methods by no means represent a complete list of external resource payment options. There are numerous other arrangements that can be made, limited only by what is agreeable to both the client and vendor. Nevertheless, we are going to limit our detailed discussion to the five above mentioned methods, including the benefits and drawbacks of each method.

Paying for hours worked is both a straightforward and convenient payment method. However, the downside of this method, there is usually no guarantee client desired quality and/or quantity levels will be met. Meaning, the vendor could deliver undesirable quality and/or insufficient quantity of service without consequences.

Although paying for incidents or events inherently satisfy quantity requirements, there is no guarantee desired quality levels will be delivered. Furthermore, just as with hourly payment method, there are typically no consequences associated with the quality of service delivered. Incidentally, since I mentioned incidents and events above, allow me to explain the difference between the two. Events apply to such things as number of invoices issued, or the number of customer service or technical support calls taken. Whereas, incidents apply to repair attempts. In other words, the number of times a technician goes to the customer site before a repair is considered successfully completed. For any number of reasons, such as the technician not having the necessary repair part at hand, multiple on-site customer visits may be required before the repair is considered completed.

Paying for completed repairs resolves the multiple customer visit issue described above. In other words, the vendor is paid *only once* for the repair resolution, regardless of how many customer visits (or incidents) may be required. That said, a repair rate is going to be higher than an incident rate. For example, if historical data reveals that it takes an average of 1.5 incidents to successfully complete a repair, the repair rate will likely be 1.5 times the incident rate. From a client's perspective, which in this case I am referring to the CSS organization, I personally prefer a repair rate over an incident rate for two reasons. First, they eliminate the risk of potentially paying for multiple otherwise unnecessary customer visits. Second, they inherently motivate repair vendors to be more efficient and cost-effective, simply because the cost of multiple customer visits rests totally on their shoulders (in a manner of speaking).

Paying for a dedicated individual(s) is another straightforward payment method. However, this too does not guarantee desired quality and/or quantity performance levels will be met. Allow me to explain myself. Naturally, when a dedicated individual is hired for a given task or project, there is a presumption predefined deliverables will be met. The fact of the matter, whether or not those deliverables are actually met is dependent on the quality and the knowledge level of the external resource brought in to do the work. The only thing that is certain with this type of arrangement, the client is locked into paying for the external resource, regardless of actual accomplishments. Therefore, a notable drawback with this payment method, the client could end up making a significant investment with no guarantee deliverables will actually be met. That is the reason this payment method realistically only makes sense for time-based deliverables. For example, an interim substitute for an internal resource that may be taking a medical or maternity leave.

The last payment method we will discuss is paying for contracted projects, which typically include milestones and completion parameters. What matters most in this type of arrangement is getting the job done right and on time. In other words, achieving deliverables that are bound by time constraints and predefined service level parameters. The most notable benefit of this payment method, it essentially guarantees the project will be done as expected and on time. Otherwise, the resource vendor will suffer the related financial consequences, meaning being paid less or not paid at all for the project.

Now I'd like to briefly turn our attention to the pros and cons of utilizing an existing internal resource to handle a specific project or assignment, assuming of course that individual possesses the required knowledge and skills. From a pros standpoint, there is generally no *real* incremental cost

141

involved when a company utilizes an existing resource. The principal reason, that individual is already included in the company payroll. Another pro, there are definitely less security and quality control concern when an internal resource is utilized. From a cons standpoint, all a manager can realistically do is specify the required project goals. Whether or not those goals are actually achieved depends on the employee's knowledge, skills, motivation and drive.

Another con is related to a newly hired internal resource that is brought on board to handle a specific project. At some point, that project will be completed. Then what happens to that resource? Sure, there may be some other projects that individual can work on. But, will they be worthwhile from a value perspective, or will they simply keep the individual busy? In some situations, company management may decide that individual is no longer needed. When that happens, they will likely be faced with a related financial challenge, specifically, separation (or severance) cost. Bottom line, there are potential risks associated with all hiring decisions, whether they are for internal or external resources. That is why all resource decisions must be handled with considerable thought, care, and foresight. Otherwise, those decisions may prove regrettable from both a human impact and business profit standpoint.

Low-cost Offshore Resources Not Always the Best Choice

Low-cost offshore resources are enticing for companies and organizations like CSS who may be struggling to compete, or simply attempting to improve profitability. On the other hand, there are inherent risks associated with offshoring, which decision makers must be mindful and prepared to confront. It's important to be aware that successful offshore solutions require a considerable amount of effort to go into the planning, design, and rollout phases. And, in order to maximize positive outcome, there must be a willingness to adjust or tweak the offshore solution after it's been rolled out.

Among the biggest challenges companies face implementing a successful offshore solution are quality control and attracting and retaining qualified resources. Quality control is usually influenced by the quality of the training, and of course, the knowledge and skill level of the offshore resources who are actually doing the work. We already discussed at length the importance of training, which the same basic principles apply to training offshore resources. Therefore, let's move on to the challenge of attracting and retaining qualified resources.

Typically, when you go into a low-cost developing country that has well-educated professional resources, you are not the only company in town looking for those resources. You are sure to find other companies competing for those same precious resources. In which case, the companies that are willing to pay the highest wages usually attract the lion's share of the resources. The primary reason, most people in developing countries are struggling to improve their basic living standards. Therefore, earned wages are of utmost importance. Furthermore, most individuals will not think twice about moving from one company to another, even for a modest wage increase. The resulting extraordinary attrition will exacerbate incremental hiring, training, and development cost that will have to be incurred on replacement resources. The more complex the position, the bigger the challenge and higher the replacement cost. So, if your company is not willing or able to deal with these challenges, which some are admittedly frustrating, offshoring will likely not be a viable solution.

There is one final point I'd like to make regarding this matter. Just as with any other support solution, the knowledge and skill level of the offshore resources brought on board matters. In which case, finding desired caliber resources in a given local market can be challenging. The primary reason, the availability of those resources is heavily influenced by local economies and especially the presence of higher education institutions that fuel supply. Bangalore, India is a perfect example of a location with abundant knowledgeable and highly skilled resources. The principal reason, they have several outstanding technical universities fueling availability. The same cannot be said for many other developing countries that offer low-cost resources. My point being, if you're planning to take advantage of an offshore support solution, be mindful of local knowledge and skill limitations that may exist. Furthermore, when supply is limited, you should expect more competition for those resources. Meaning, you should be prepared to pay competitively higher wages.

At this point, I'd like to share an example of an offshore support quality challenge, which I made reference to earlier. A few years back, I joined a BU that was leveraging offshore financial resources to support USA based contracted services deals. Like most businesses who are constantly looking for ways to lower cost and improve profitability, this organization decided to switch from local to offshore financial analysts. Frankly, the solution was doomed to failure from the very beginning for two reasons.

First, training the offshore resources was the responsibility of an already overburdened USA based financial analyst. Considering all of the other important day-to-day responsibilities this individual had, his plate was already full (so to speak). Therefore, remotely training people from half way around the globe was simply not a priority. Second, just like most things that are done with lack of sufficient time and marginal interest, the resulting training turned out to be grossly inadequate. In retrospect, once I learned about this individual's time struggle, I'd say the outcome was predictable. The blame for failure did not rest with that individual or the offshore resources. Management was clearly at fault for not committing sufficient resources to a decision they made.

Vendors Must Be Accountable for End-client Deliverables

From a best practices standpoint, most external resource agreements should include clearly outlined deliverables and performance goals. When external resources are hired by a middleman like a CSS organization, the deliverables and performance goals CSS is accountable to the end-client should also be reflected in the agreement between the external resource vendor and CSS. That way, both parties share responsibility for achieving end-client deliverables, as well as the risk of incurring potential non-performance penalties.

I have seen cases in which contracts with third-party resource vendors were loosely defined and less stringent than the deliverables CSS was accountable to the end-client. Worse yet, I've seen other cases in which there was no mention of end-client deliverables in the agreement between the resource vendor and CSS. Under either of the given circumstances, if the vendor is reliable and provides high quality resources, there is no harm done. On the other hand, if the resource vendor is not reliable and end-client deliverables are not met, the situation can become costly for CSS. In extreme situations, CSS may even run the risk of losing the end-client. Bottom line, it behooves all parties involved to utilize very clear and unambiguous contract language outlining responsibilities and accountabilities. Furthermore, it's always best when everyone involved in end-client deliverables are focused on achieving the same results and have some skin in the game.

Part III

Managing the Financials

Chapter 13

Managing the CSS P&L

I'd like to start our discussion regarding CSS P&L management with a foundational question that must first always be answered. Should CSS be treated as a profit center or cost center? In this case, we are assuming CSS is a horizontal BU inside a multi-product line company. Wherein, each product line is led by a vertical BU executive. From a reporting structure standpoint, the CSS executive and the Product BU executives would all typically report directly to the company president or chief operating officer (COO). The only difference between their responsibilities, the Product BU executives would be singularly focused on the success of their respective product line. Whereas, the CSS executive would provide service and support to each of the Product BUs.

Companies that have an internal CSS organization have to deal with some unique accounting requirements. Specifically, in a cost center structure, they would deal with warranty cost relief and funding for support functions such as Customer Service, Technical Support, and others. There are several different warranty cross-charge and funding methodologies that can be used, which we will discuss in detail in the upcoming *Cost Center* section. On the other hand, in a profit center structure, CSS financial interaction with the Product BUs is essentially limited to revenue sharing. The reason being, CSS is managed as a standalone organization that is responsible for contributing profit to the company, just as the Product BUs are. Although revenue sharing is relatively straightforward, we will discuss it is more detail in the upcoming *Profit Center* section.

Incidentally, both organizational structures allow CSS to produce revenue that is generated from extended warranty and service contract sales. Therefore, a cost center structure is typically not pure cost, per se. In most cases, CSS will produce its own P&L. The principal difference between cost center and profit center, in a cost center structure most of the accounting affecting the Product BUs will be reflected in the cost portion of the CSS P&L. Whereas, in a profit center structure, most of the Product BU related accounting will be reflected in the revenue portion of the CSS P&L.

Before we get into the profit center and cost center details, I'd like to personally weigh in on the matter. In my opinion, profit center structure will generally produce better results. The principal reason, there is inherently more financial accountability when managers are responsible for producing gross margin than when they are essentially subsidized by other organizations.

Profit Center Structure

As mentioned earlier, CSS profit center accounting essentially involves revenue sharing with the Product BUs. There are two primary methods revenue sharing can be handled. The first is sharing a percentage of the revenue, and the second is sharing an absolute dollar amount. The percentage method works as described in the following example. A Product BU sells a product to a customer for $1,000, which the BU is financially responsible for warranty service and support. Let's assume historical warranty service and support cost for that product is roughly $80. In which case, the Product BU would likely transfer approximately 10% of the revenue, or $100, to the CSS BU to cover warranty cost plus a reasonable $20 profit.

Sharing an absolute dollar amount accomplishes the same basic results. The only difference, the agreement between the Product BUs and CSS is based on dollar value rather than a percentage of revenue. Regardless of the method used, the percentage rates or dollar amounts will likely vary based on different products or product lines, as reflected in the Product BUs and CSS negotiations during the annual budgeting process. Adjustment can subsequently be made for extraordinary circumstances, such as a newly launched product that is deemed to be a *lemon*. Next, I'd like to point out a few notable pros and cons associated with a profit center structure.

Notable Pros:

1. Being self-sufficient will usually produce better overall results.
2. Motivates incented CSS P&L managers to do their best.
3. A CSS BU that is accountable for profit will usually be viewed as being equally important to the Product BUs. Whereas, a subsidized CSS may be viewed as being subservient to the Product BUs.

Notable Cons:

1. With more accountability typically comes higher risk of failure.

2. If the profit objective is not achieved, there will be no one to blame except CSS management.

3. The risk of experiencing extraordinary warranty service and support cost rests totally with CSS, with the possible exception of special consideration being given to products that are deemed to be *lemons*.

To be clear, the above list of pros and cons is not intended to portray an all-inclusive list. Instead, the depicted items represent some of the more obvious pros and cons associated with a CSS profit center structure.

Cost Center Structure

Accounting for a CSS cost center structure is more involved than profit center accounting. As mentioned earlier, cost center accounting deals with warranty cost relief, as well as funding for support functions such as Customer Service, Technical Support, and others. There are a couple of common methods used to handle warranty cross-charges from CSS to the Product BUs. Likewise, there are a couple of common methods used to handle funding for Customer Service, Technical Support and other functions. We're going to talk about those various methods shortly. In addition, I will point out a few notable pros and cons of going with a cost center structure.

Let's start with warranty cross-charges, which are usually based on a per-incident labor rate plus parts consumption cost. The per incident labor rate typically varies by product model or product line. And, the parts consumption cost is generally derived from the company's standard cost system.

Incidentally, an alternative to incident-based cost relief, is repair based cost relief. Allow me to explain the difference between the two. An incident occurs each time a field technician is dispatched. In other words, if there are three dispatches for the same problem, there would be three separate warranty cost charges from CSS to the Product BU. Whereas, repair-based cost relief only allows CSS to make a single warranty charge to the Product BU, regardless of the number of times field technicians are dispatched. So, you might be wondering, how does repair based cost relief actually work? Let's assume the historical number of incidents/repair is 1.5, meaning the average repair requires 1.5 incidents. Let's assume further, the incident rate for a particular product category is $100. That would make the repair cost relief rate $150. There is a hidden benefit going with repair rates. Specifically, CSS would be motivated to work smarter by minimizing the number of field technician dispatches.

A less commonly used method handling warranty cross-charges is actual repair time multiplied by the technician's fully burdened labor rate, plus parts consumption cost. You may recall, we previously discussed fully burdened labor rates, including how they are typically calculated by technician job codes.

With regard to funding the support organizations, I would say a fixed annual dollar amount represents the most commonly used method. That way, CSS can staff Customer Service and Technical Support according to the Product BU's desired support levels. Incidentally, the staffing level usually correlates with a standard performance measure, typically, *average speed to answer*. In other words, the average amount of time customers have to wait to get a live agent on the phone. Some Product BU executives may not be particularly concerned with how long customers have to wait in the call queue. Whereas, other BU executives may be willing to pay for extra support staffing to ensure customers do not have to wait long in the call queue. Other times, funding decisions are more so influenced by what the Product BU can afford rather than achieving a desired performance level.

A less common method used to fund support functions such as Customer Service and Technical support is based on actual calls handles. In this case, at the end of each month there would be an accounting of actual calls handled, which would be multiplied by previously agreed per call rates between Product BU and CSS management.

There are several other methods that can be used to handle warranty cross-charges and support organizations funding, limited only by what is agreeable to both Product BU and CSS management. Next, let's talk about a few notable pros and cons associated with a cost center structure.

Notable Pros:

1. Product BUs largely provide a safety net for CSS, which protects CSS from performance failure.
2. CSS management is less accountable for achieving financial success.
3. If the profit objective is not achieved, CSS can partially blame Product BUs for their failure, pointing to the following excuses: warranty cross-charge rates are too low; funding for CSS support organizations is too low; actual product failures are higher than planned, etc.

Notable Cons:

1. Product BUs largely provide a safety net for CSS, which may otherwise *mask* poor CSS performance.
2. A subsidized CSS BU may be viewed as being subservient to the Product BUs.
3. Does little to motivate CSS managers to do their best.

Here again, the above list of pros and cons is not intended to portray an all-inclusive list. However, the depicted items represent some of the more obvious pros and cons associated with a CSS cost center structure.

To reiterate a point I made earlier, in my opinion, a profit center structure will almost always produce better overall results. That opinion is formulated from personal experience, as controller for a CSS organization who was responsible for co-leading a successful cost center to profit center conversion effort.

Reliable P&Ls Start and End with Financial Integrity

The single most important quality regarding reliable financial performance reporting is integrity. We have all heard the old adage, *garbage in garbage out.* Truer words could not be said regarding P&L integrity. Without integrity, P&Ls are not only misleading, they are potentially downright dangerous. The reason being, many business decisions are influenced by P&L results. Data integrity is not something that accidentally happens. It must be engrained into the company culture. For example, as mundane as account coding may be, it is a common source of data integrity issues. Therefore, businesses must ensure employees are properly trained on account coding dos and don'ts. There are of course several other factors that affect data integrity. Next, we're going to talk about common factors that affect P&L accuracy and reliability, starting with those that affect revenue, followed by those that affect cost.

Customer billing is unquestionably the most significant factor that affects revenue. In which case, the accuracy of Portfolio and Regional P&Ls are only as good as the customer name and number coding on billing transactions. As obvious is that may appear to be, it's a problem in most large companies. Why, you might be wondering? Throughout my professional career, I have worked in four major international corporations. I have never seen what I would characterize as a streamlined and efficient customer master data management process. In fact, I have seen the direct opposite.

For the same customer, there could be as many as a half dozen or more name variations and corresponding customer numbers assigned in the customer master database. For example, for General Electric Company, there could be the following name variations: General Electric Company, GE Co., General Electric, GE, etc. You get the idea. Which of those names is selected by the sales order administrator, including the possibility that she may create an entirely new customer name and number, which is based on the sales order paperwork in front of her, matters from a P&L reporting integrity standpoint.

Simply put, account coding errors typically occur because of inadequate training and lacking or loosely defined customer master admin processes. Incidentally, it's important to understand, account coding inaccuracy has no effect on the total company P&L. However, it certainly does affect Portfolio and Regional P&Ls. Furthermore, if/when it's determined a P&L reporting error has occurred, costly and cumbersome manual intervention will likely be required to correct the reporting error (as in manual journal entries). Obviously, this type of problem can be avoided if there is more care and attention applied to the upfront administrative processes.

Other revenue related financial integrity issues may occur as a result of sales order and billing data entry errors, such as applying the wrong billing rate or wrong discount rate. Suffice to say, most revenue integrity issues are the result of erroneous administrative actions that relate to customer master data, sales order processing, and billing. Furthermore, P&L reporting errors may be due to how deferred revenue is handled. For example, erroneously recognizing an entire annual billing amount as earned revenue, instead of deferring 11 of the 12 months revenue. The issues we just discussed are among the most common problems that affect revenue integrity.

With regard to cost integrity, I will share three examples that commonly occur in CSS organizations. First, the accuracy of direct labor and parts usage charges as reflected in the Field Service Management System. In this case, the wrong labor hours may have been reported or wrong consumed part number referenced, resulting in erroneous charges to the

Portfolio or Regional P&Ls. Remember, the quality of reported data is only as good as the accuracy of the input. Since field technicians are human, and humans are prone to make some mistakes, these types of problems will surely occur from time to time. Hence, it's up to the P&L manager to routinely review cross-charge reports for accuracy. Some P&L owners take the shortcut approach, meaning just look at the report totals. If the totals are in the expected ballpark, there is no further review or analysis done, which can turn out to be a costly mistake. The reason being, there could be a few erroneous charges buried in the detail, which will never be discovered.

The second example has to do with the integrity of cost assigned to P&Ls. Let's assume you are responsible for a portfolio that includes 10 major accounts, which individual P&Ls are produced for each account. Let's assume further, in additional to receiving service from internal resources, those major accounts are also supported by a third-party service provider. Since internal service resources utilize the Field Service Management System, there are virtually no issues getting the right amount of internal service cost to the right Major Account P&L. On the other hand, getting the right amount of third-party service cost assigned to those P&Ls can be problematic. Especially if those charges are being allocated instead of distributed on an actual transaction basis.

One common cost allocation method is to base the charges on the percentage of *total revenue* each account represents. Another method is to base it on the percentage of *total cost* incurred to support each major account. Of course, there are other ways to allocate cost, but these two methods are among the most common. Regardless of what allocation method is used, they all boil down to some sort of so-called *peanut butter spread*, which is imperfect at best. Consequently, it may result in relatively inaccurate Major Account P&Ls, which may affect business decisions that are made regarding those accounts. Bottom line, the more cost is allocated, the less accurate and reliable you should expect impacted P&Ls to be.

The third and final example of a cost integrity issue we will discuss has to do with miscoded Purchase Orders (POs), a problem I have seen accidentally occur on several occasions. Oftentimes, the PO originator does not reside in the cost center the products or services being purchased are finally intended. Let's assume the PO originator is an administrator in the local CSS region office. Let's assume further, external resources are temporarily required to support a particular major account, which has its own designated cost center. A common problem that occurs, the regional administrator will inadvertently code the PO with his own cost center instead of the major account cost center. Therefore, when vendor payments are made against that PO, the charges end up in the region cost center instead of the intended major account cost center. If and when that problem is subsequently discovered, the only way to fix it is with manual intervention, meaning reclassify the cost via a journal entry. Worse yet is when those problems remain unnoticed, simply because the Regional P&L owner does not take the time to review monthly cost detail reports. In which case, cost permanently remains in the wrong cost center, resulting in misstated P&Ls. Plain and simple, the best way to prevent this type of problem from manifesting is for the P&L owner or his designee to routinely review monthly cost detail reports.

Understanding Transaction Source Data

You can't fix something you don't understand. That is to say, you cannot effectively manage and control profitability if you don't understand the related transaction source data. Let's first talk about the different sources of services financial data. Essentially, there are three sources, listed in the order of preference: 1) integrated reporting databases, 2) individual application system databases, and 3) spreadsheets and manual transactions such as journal entries. In an ideal situation, a company would have an integrated reporting database with robust capability, from which they could pull detailed financial transaction reports, as well as various other standard and ad hoc reports. Incidentally, the reporting database would be routinely updated with transaction data from a number of independent business application system feeds.

The next best way of getting to the source data is directly from independent business application system databases. In other words, this would be a non-integrated solution that would require more work pulling the data together and making sense out of the fragmented reporting. The least desirable way of getting to the source data is from makeshift spreadsheets and individual manual transactions such as journal entries. Obviously, the second and third methods are not nearly as desirable and efficient as the first. The fact of the matter, not every business can afford to have an integrated reporting database solution. Particularly small and medium size companies who are often struggling with mere existence. Nevertheless, the more automated and integrated the database solution, the more efficient and better quality will be the reported data.

Incidentally, having transaction level data available from whichever of the above-mentioned sources does not necessarily mean it will be understood by the report recipients and that something worthwhile will be done with the data. Keeping in mind that we are discussing financial implications of business transactions, what we're really talking about is understanding how those transactions positively or negatively impact revenue and cost.

Let's consider an example that impacts revenue, in which a Major Account P&L owner is preparing a total year revenue forecast. Month 3 just closed, which includes a

$75,000 one-time billing spike. The spike was due to 5 months retroactive service billing for devices that were added toward the end of the prior fiscal year. Given the typical paperwork processing lag time that occurs in most businesses, this scenario is not at all uncommon. In any case, one of the most common mistakes that occurs forecasting a recurring revenue stream like service is simply doing run-rate forecasting. Needless to say, this mindless approach will more often than not lead to inaccurate and unreliable forecasts. Next, I'm going to run through some numbers, so please stay with me.

Let's assume the normal service run-rate billing for this major account was $100,000/month prior to the one-time retroactive billing adjustment. If the forecast is done properly, the total year revenue estimate would be $1,410,000, which would be calculated as follows: $100,000 for each month 1 and 2, plus $175,000 for month 3, plus $115,000 for each month 4 – 12. The reason for the $115,000 future monthly amount, the $75,000 five months back billing would have added $15,000/month to the revenue base. On the other hand, if the forecast is done improperly (based on year-to-date run-rate), the total year forecast would be $1,500,000, which would have been calculated as follows: $375,000 for months 1 – 3 combined, plus $125,000 for each month 4 – 12. The $125,000/month was derived from dividing actual year-to-date revenue of $375,000 by 3. This erroneous approach would result in $90,000 forecasting error, simply because the P&L owner does know how to properly utilize transaction source data.

Now let's consider an example that impacts cost. This example has to do with a questionable labor charge from the Field Service Management System. As P&L owner for a major account, this individual has access to labor cross-charge reports that contain the following details: service technician names, hours worked, parts used, cross-charge amounts, and

160

more. Let's assume the P&L owner is either too busy with other matters, or simply does not understand how to interpret and leverage labor cross-charge reports. Nevertheless, ignoring or not understanding how to leverage those reports can prove costly from a P&L standpoint. How, you might wonder? I cannot tell you the number of times I have seen two predominant error types occur that are related to technician labor charges. Neither of those errors done intentionally by the person entering data into the Field Service Management System. Nonetheless, the labor cross-charge errors ultimately resulted in misstated P&Ls.

Now let's talk about those two predominant labor reporting error types. The first is a cost center coding error. Meaning, labor is charged to the wrong major account cost center. Think about it. You have a sizable field service organization with hundreds of technicians charging time (cost) to accounts they support. On any given week a technician will typically service several different customers. Therefore, it's not hard to imagine how a non-intentional cost center coding error could occur. Hence, if the P&L owner does not review the labor cross-charge report, an unintentional coding error could easily slip through the cracks and adversely affect his P&L.

The second predominant error that occurs is the so-called *fat finger error.* In this case, let's assume an intended 4 hours input was accidentally entered as 40 hours. As the saying goes, what's an extra zero amongst friends? Let's do the math and see. Let's assume the fully burdened labor rate for the individual reporting the labor is $100/hour, that fat finger error just cost the P&L owner an additional $3,600 (36 hours @ $100/hour). This is another example of what would have been time well spent by the P&L owner (or designee) who was on the receiving end of the erroneous charge. Here again, this example demonstrates that taking the time to review source data reports can certainly be worthwhile. Listen, I've been there. So, I am very familiar with the everyday struggles a P&L owner faces. It's a constant juggling act, deciding what to work on and what to ignore. In most cases, a P&L owner has more things to do than time available in the workday. However, somehow or other, she must either find the time or assign someone who understands source data to routinely review and address issues that are uncovered from operations management reports.

Negotiating Budgets with Product BU Management

Earlier, I briefly made reference to the annual budgeting process between the Product BUs and CSS. At this point, I'd like to discuss the budget negotiation process in more details. First of all, I'd like to say this process can be quite lengthy (meaning take several months) and be rather testy and frustrating. At least for individuals sitting on the CSS side of the negotiating table, which I personally sat many times. The reason I say that, the more arrogant is the Product BU executive and his controller, the more challenging the negotiation process. I say *arrogant* because there is oftentimes a misguided attitude that the Product BU is doing CSS a favor allowing them to service and support their products and customers. Hence, the budget negotiations process can be a recurring annual struggle for CSS management to come to agreement with those particular Product BU executives. Instead, the relationship between the two parties should be one of mutual respect, with one organization responsible for providing products and the other delivering service and support for those products/customers.

The fact of the matter, year after year, Product BUs expect to progressively receive faster, cheaper, and better support from CSS for lower cost. Granted, investing in improved service and support tools and technology can make that possible, as can improved quality products. However, there are limits to how much improvement can be made possible, while simultaneously lowering cost. Nevertheless, best in class companies should rightfully expect their internal service organization to provide support to the Product BUs at competitive cost. In other words, at the same or lower cost than is available from external service providers. The only benefit an internal service organization should have over external service providers is *right of first refusal.* Basically, that means being the only player that is given *open bid* access, allowing them an opportunity to beat the competition. Whereas, competing external vendors are confined to a standard *closed bidding* process.

Billable Service Contracts

Before we get into the detailed discussion regarding billable service contracts, there a few points I'd like to make regarding terminology. *Billable service contracts* refer to any and all billable coverage options a customer may elect to purchase beyond the manufacturer's standard warranty. There are two labels commonly used for these billable services, *extended warranty* and *service contracts*. Unfortunately, standardized terminology does not exist. In which case, depending on the company offering the services, the two labels are used interchangeably. However, for this book, I'm going to make a clear distinction between the two. Extended warranty provides customers higher level coverage options *during the warranty period.* Whereas, service contracts provide customers a variety of service and support options after the warranty period expires.

Let's start our detailed discussion by talking about service marketing. As with any marketing organization, service marketing is responsible for developing strategies and creating accompanying information (brochures, etc.) that promote the sale of service contracts. As mentioned above, there are typically two different types of billable service contracts. First, contracts that simply extend standard warranty coverage beyond the warranty period. Second, contracts that provide service coverage above and beyond standard warranty. For example, provide four hours versus eight hours standard warranty response, in addition to a variety of other billable service and support options.

Now let's talk about selling those service contracts. There are essentially three different methods a CSS organization can sell service contracts. The first is at the product point of sale. This method is both common and cost-effective, since it simply involves adding a line item to the customer's product invoice or bill of sale. In which case, there is virtually no incremental selling cost involved. The second method is utilizing a dedicated CSS sales team, which would only be cost justifiable in a significant size CSS business unit. The third method is leveraging the company's general sales force, which is primarily responsible for product sales. In this case, I will tell you from personal experience, it may be challenging getting attention from the company's general sales force. The reason being, sales incentives on service contracts are typically significantly lower than incentives on relatively higher priced product sales. Hence, given the choice, a salesperson will almost always spend more time and effort on product sales than service contract sales for one reason, maximize her sales incentive compensation.

Given this common dilemma, there are two things the company can do to sell more service contracts. One, offer more gracious sales incentive for service contracts. In other words, if product sale incentive is 5%, make the service contract sale incentive 7.5% or 10%. The reality of the situation, if you want to get a salesperson's attention, it must be done via sales incentives. The other way of getting a salesperson's attention is by mandating, let's say, 50% of product sales must be accompanied by corresponding service contract sales. In other words, the only way a salesperson can maximize her incentive compensation is by meeting or beating the service contract percentage goal. Next, let's talk about extended warranty contracts and the various types of other service contracts in more detail.

Extended Warranty Contracts

I'd like to start by reiterating my definition of extended warranty contracts. They provide customers higher level coverage options during the warranty period. From a profitability standpoint, extended warranty contracts can be lucrative, depending on two primary conditions. First and foremost, the level of quality and reliability that is built into the product and second the product serviceability, which we discussed the details in Chapter 1. The other reason these contracts tend to be profitable, unless the company is dealing with a *lemon*, most reasonably built products will experience relatively fewer service issues during the warranty period. It's usually after the warranty period expires that imperfections and wear and tear issues start popping up more and more in moderate to poor quality built products.

From a billing standpoint, extended warranty contracts are commonly billed in advance. Meaning, they are generally billed on an annual basis. As discussed in the Chapter 8, accounting for advanced billing involves deferring revenue recognition. To reiterate what was stated earlier, generally accepted accounting principles require earned revenue and corresponding cost to be recognized during the same accounting period. Meaning, only the earned portion of revenue can be reflected in the current period P&L. In which case, if a customer is billed $1,200 for a full year extended warranty contract, the company cannot recognize the entire billed amount as earned revenue. Instead, revenue must be recognized over a 12 month period at $100/month to match incurred monthly cost.

Post-warranty Service Contracts

Here again, I'd like to start by reiterating what was stated earlier regarding service contracts. These contracts serve one of two purposes. First, provide customers the same level service as standard warranty for an extended period of time. Second, provide customers billable options that are over and above standard warranty coverage.

Just as extended warranty contracts can be lucrative, so too can be service contracts, depending on the same two primary conditions, quality and reliability built into the product and serviceability. On the other hand, there is a higher probability of experiencing more repair activity with service contracts, especially for moderate to poor quality built products, which tend to fail more after the warranty period expires. In other words, as those products age, quality shortcomings will typically become increasingly evident. In those situations, service contracts are likely to put a strain on profit rather than positively contribute to profit.

Compared to extended warranty contracts, a higher percentage of service contracts are billed monthly instead of in advance. Nevertheless, there are many situations service contracts are billed quarterly or annually, which requires deferred revenue recognition treatment, as described above.

Time and Material Service

Time and material mean you are servicing a non-contracted customer. From a revenue and profit standpoint, time and material service is typically very lucrative. The principal reason, customers are billed at list price for labor and parts.

Incidentally, the difference between time and material and contracted services, the former will only generate revenue and profit when repair incident occurs. Whereas, with contract services, revenue and profit contribution is highest when there are no repair incidents involved.

Service Contracts for Other Vendor Products

Since service infrastructure typically represents a substantial investment, service organizations often look for ways to help recover some of that investment by offering services for other vendor products. For example, in an integrated IT environment, it's common for a client to have multiple vendor products co-existing in the same physical location. When those situations exist, it may present one or more of the service vendors an opportunity to convince the client that having a single vendor support their entire environment would be best. For the client, one of the primary benefits of having a single service provider, it essentially eliminates the possibility of vendor finger pointing when something goes wrong in the integrated environment. I will tell you from personal experience, there are few things that are more frustrating for the client than vendor finger pointing.

For the vendor, one of the benefits is maximizing utilization of their service infrastructure, including their field technicians. Another benefit, of course, is increasing revenue and profit opportunity. However, I must warn you, there is a downside in these situations. Specifically, getting access to other vendor proprietary spare parts at reasonable prices can be problematic. After all, it's a competitive world out there. No vendor is going to make it easy for other vendors to take support business away from them.

Chapter 14

Maximizing Profitability

Business drivers mean different things to different people, and in a broad sense can include any number of both internal and external factors. In the upcoming discussion, our focus will primarily be on internal business drivers that impact a CSS P&L. As P&L owner, if you do nothing to influence those drivers, like it or not, you will live with the resulting consequences. On the other hand, managing those drivers will almost certainly result in improved P&L performance. To be clear, we are talking about business drivers that maximize revenue and/or minimize cost.

Noteworthy, the order in which we will discuss these drivers, more or less, follow the order the book has been written, rather than some priority order. Thus, we're going to start with cost drivers followed by revenue drivers. Furthermore, since this chapter will address most of the key areas covered in the detailed writing, it will also serve as a summary of best practices takeaways.

Managing Cost Business Drivers

Since CSS is more so a cost producing than a sales generating organization, there are abundantly more cost drivers than revenue drivers that can be managed to improve profitability. Below is a list of notable cost drivers, which will be followed by a detailed explanation of each item:

1. Products designed for serviceability cost less to support.

2. Maximize Customer Service efficiency and cost effectiveness.

3. Maximize Technical Support efficiency and cost effectiveness.

4. Implement a user-friendly knowledge base.

5. Deliver contracted service level (not significantly more or less).

6. Maximize remote resolutions while minimizing field dispatches.

7. Maximize coverage area at the lowest possible cost.

8. Minimize trial and error parts replacement.

9. Maximize customer assisted repairs.

10. Implement an optimal parts logistics strategy.

11. Implement an optimal repair strategy.

12. Implement an optimal refurbishment strategy.

13. Cost effectively manage clients.

14. Cost effectively justify human resources.

15. Maximize direct labor resource utilization.

16. Minimize use of marginal value indirect labor resources.

17. Effectively manage and control resource vendor cost.

1) Products designed for serviceability cost less to support:

From a design and manufacturing standpoint, it's generally more costly to build products that are easily and efficiently serviced. However, from a service cost standpoint, the direct opposite is true. Performing routine preventive and remedial service on products that are designed with serviceability in mind is certainly less costly. Although there is a little more upfront cost involved, building serviceable products can potentially save the company a great deal of post-launch aggravation and cost, if those products require an extraordinary amount of remedial service.

I can tell you from personal experience, doing product recalls or on-site service sweeps are exceedingly costly and often have disastrous effects on customer satisfaction. I'm inclined to say, it's one of the surest ways of jeopardizing customer loyalty. And, as virtually everyone in business is aware, customer loyalty is generally hard to earn and easy to lose. Moreover, poor quality product will almost certainly adversely influence loyalty.

Regrettably, the value of design for serviceability is not well understood and appreciated by many product companies. The principal reason, it's difficult to absolutely assess the resulting benefit. Although that may be true, there are seemingly endless examples of costly product recalls and/or on-site service sweeps that have been required to repair defective products. When those corrective actions are required, there is an enormous cost difference between servicing easily accessible product components versus those that are difficult to get to and replace.

2) Maximize Customer Service efficiency and cost effectiveness:

How efficient and cost-effective a Customer Service function operates is influenced by three predominant factors. First, having an organizational structure that is built around meeting customer needs. Second, having internal processes and workflows that seamlessly integrate with other organizations that work closely with Customer Service such as: Technical

Support, Field Operations, Business Operations, etc. Third, continuously training employees to enhance the overall knowledge and skills of the team.

Besides people related cost, one of the most significant cost items associated with Customer Service Centers is telephone expense, since agents are constantly on the phone and customers are commonly provided toll-free numbers. That said, implementing a call-back process, instead of having customers waiting on hold in the call queue, is both cost-effective and a welcome option by most customers, on the condition they maintain their position in the call queue.

Although there are some people who are happy and professionally satisfied being a customer service agent, there are many others who consider the work mundane, and don't stay in those positions very long. In which case, managers are often challenged finding ways to keep the agents happy and satisfied with their work. There are a number of things that can be done to accomplish that objective. One of the biggies is empowerment. There are few things that employees dislike more than having to obtain supervisor approval regarding matters that would otherwise be considered routine actions and/or decisions.

My advice is, empower the agents to the extent it is reasonably possible. Sure, some mistakes will be made. But, providing constructive feedback and/or focused training that address those mistakes will almost always produce better results than needless close supervision. Furthermore, taking that route will almost certainly be less costly than constantly having to rotate new people through the organization. You may recall, in the detailed section on subject, I provided an example of how we allowed customer service agents to handle rudimentary technical support calls. Not only did that change prove to be an effective motivational tool, it also helped keep several of the customer service agents in their positions longer.

3) Maximize Technical Support efficiency and cost effectiveness:

In moderate to large product companies, Technical Support organizations are typically broken down by product line. Whereas, in smaller companies, the same set-up generally does not make economic sense. The reasons being, optimal organizational design often comes down to economies of scale and the all-important question, which design will produce the lowest cost per call? Hence, if your company produces three product lines and has 75 agents on board, designating roughly 25 agents to support each product line would be sensible.

On the other hand, if your company produces three product lines and only has three agents on board, each trained and designated to support a single product line, that would likely *not* be sensible. The principal reason, depending on the issues and challenges with a given product line, one agent could be overwhelmed with calls while the other two are largely sitting idle. Therefore, having all three agents trained to support all three product lines would make more sense. That way, you would have built-in flexibility to shift agents focus to where they are needed most. Although training cost would be greater, the payback, in terms of added flexibility, will most likely outweigh the incremental training cost.

In addition to being organized around product lines, there are a couple of other viable organizational options. The first, have a single group of agents support all three product lines. However, as mentioned earlier, this structure will drive up training cost, which is the reason it only makes economic sense for small support organizations. The second option, create a hybrid structure, which is primarily made up of single product agents and secondarily multiple product agents. For example, roughly 80% of the agents would be permanently assigned to designated product lines, while the other 20% float in and out of product lines as needed. Here again, training cost incurred on the multiple product agents would be greater. However, the ability to fluidly assign agents to product lines that are experiencing the highest call volumes will almost certainly justify the additional training cost.

Many companies, especially technology companies, provide customers 24/7 support. And, in several of those cases, they adopt a cost-effective strategy known as *Follow the Sun*. Meaning, for a USA based company, they would use local technical support agents to provide daytime support, let's say, from 8AM – 8PM local time. And, for after-hours support, from 8PM – 8AM, they would use offshore resources that are located ½ way around the world (for example India), where it would be daytime locally.

Just as with Customer Service Centers, besides people related cost, the second most significant cost associated with Technical Support Centers is telephone expense. Once again, the reason being, agents are constantly on the phone, and customers are oftentimes provided toll-free numbers. In order to minimize telephone expense, in most cases, it would make a great deal of sense to adopt a call-back instead of call waiting process. As mentioned earlier, such a process can be cost-effective and be a welcomed choice by many customers, as long as they will maintain their position in the call queue.

From both a process excellence and cost effectiveness standpoint, many companies adopt a tiered technical support structure. Typically, there are three tiers of support: L1, L2, and L3. The L1 team consists of generalists who handle common and least complicated technical problems. They represent the largest team, which typically resolve most of the technical support calls with the help of scripts and an internal knowledge base. The L2 team consists of more highly skilled and highly paid technicians who typically handle escalated L1 calls. And, the L3 agents, who are oftentimes members of the hardware or software development team, will handle rarely escalated L2 calls. The principal benefit of tiered support, it helps to minimize the average cost/call by having the lower cost L1 agents handle the bulk of the technical calls.

4) Implement a user-friendly knowledge base:

From a cost effectiveness standpoint, one of the best investments a CSS organization can make is creating a robust and user-friendly knowledge base. Think about it. Every time a customer helps himself with information posted on the knowledge base, that's one less call the Technical Support organization has to handle. Incidentally, there are two types of customers that seek technical support. First, you have people who are inherently uncomfortable and, in some cases, intimidated by technology. In those cases, you could have the most robust and user-friendly knowledge base in the world, and those people would still not access your knowledge base. On the other hand, you have tech savvy clients who are comfortable with self-help and, in many cases, prefer not to have to deal with people. Those individuals will almost certainly welcome a knowledge base, which will contribute to lowering call volume and overall support cost.

All things considered, a web accessible knowledge base is a smart and a worthwhile investment for most modern-day companies. The reason being, people are increasingly becoming more comfortable accessing the web for everyday personal and business needs, including self-help knowledge bases.

5) Deliver contracted service level (not significantly more or less):

Delivering service that is significantly above or below the contracted level can represent a *double whammy*. As will be mentioned below in the revenue drivers sections, the implications of over delivering could very well mean potential revenue loss, if the higher service level is truly required by the client. Furthermore, from a cost standpoint, over delivering represents an unnecessary incremental cost. Whereas, under delivering can temporally lower your operating cost, but you will run the risk of upsetting and potentially losing customers.

Bottom line, materially over and under delivering is equally bad for business. On the one hand, being overly petty with contracted clients, waving the signed contract to point out insignificant billable service exclusions, is not smart. Neither is incurring unnecessary delivery cost. Staying within a reasonable and respectful middle ground with contracted clients will always serve you best, from both a relationship and profitability standpoint.

6) Maximize remote resolutions while minimizing field dispatches:

Without question, the most significant cost item in a CSS organization that provides on-site service is field operations cost. Therefore, the organization must do everything reasonably possible to minimize dispatching on-site technicians. One of the most cost-effective ways of accomplishing that goal is staffing the front-end process, namely, the Diagnostics and Dispatch Center, with highly skilled technicians. The principal objective being, remotely diagnose and resolve as many problems as possible without dispatching technicians. Unfortunately, the agents in those front-end positions often do nothing more than take customer calls and dispatch technicians, which is costly and oftentimes totally unnecessary.

Instead of staffing those centers with low level call takers, they should be staffed with well-trained and highly skilled technicians. Of course, that would increase the operating cost of the center. However, the payback from avoiding unnecessary on-site dispatches is almost guaranteed to be greater. Evolving from a simple call taking to a remote diagnostics and resolution mindset will be challenging. Especially if it involves having to physically relocate some of your best field technicians to the Diagnostics and Dispatch Center. Incidentally, in order to accomplish that goal, you have to be flexible on two fronts. First, offer sought after individuals attractive compensation packages, potentially accompanied by performance incentives. Second, allow them to work remotely instead of physically relocating to the Diagnostics and Dispatch Center, if that is one of the conditions they demand.

Noteworthy, employee attitude regarding relocation has dramatically changed over the past couple of decades. Getting people to uproot away from their family and friends is a big deal nowadays. Furthermore, technological advances have made working virtually seamlessly possible in many cases. Bottom line, being reasonably flexible with your employees will ultimately serve you best.

7) Maximize coverage area at the lowest possible cost:

There are a number of different strategies field operations can adopt to maximize coverage area. How cost-effective each of those strategies is largely depends on the distribution of the installed customer base and the size and scope of the CSS organization.

Although unrealistic, if all of your customers are concentrated in a single geographic location, you don't have to worry about maximizing coverage area. On the other hand, if your customers are widely dispersed, you definitely need to be concerned about how to cost effectively provide on-site service to all those customers. In most cases, large companies typically have a combination of concentrated and remote customer sites they have to service. So, the question becomes, what is the best coverage strategy in those situations? The answer is, it depends on the size and scope of the internal CSS organization.

A typical CSS organization that is fairly substantial in size and scope would likely have adequate internal coverage capability to service urban and business campus environments. However, they would most likely be thinly spread in suburban and rural areas. In which case, they would typically rely on third-party companies to service those remote customers. What I just described is precisely the *hybrid* coverage model many companies adopt. The reason being, there is no infrastructure cost required to support those remote customers. Furthermore, this model minimizes lost productivity resulting from extraordinary travel time, as well as accompanying travel cost. On the other hand, third-party service companies often thrive on remote support because they commonly service multiple manufacturers' products in the local areas.

8) Minimize trial and error parts replacement:

There are a few different ways of isolating and dealing with remedial service issues. The two I want to address, from a cost/benefit standpoint, are diagnostics based versus trial-and-error parts replacement. Given the required tools and properly skilled technicians, the most cost-effective way of honing in on a problem is via remote diagnostics. Alternatively, diagnostics can be done at the customer's site, but that will necessitate dispatching a field technician. If an on-site repair is ultimately required, the technician would have had to be dispatched anyway. Therefore, there is no additional service cost involved. On the other hand, if the problem could have been successfully resolved remotely, dispatching the field technician would have turned out to be a waste of time and money.

By far, the most costly way of dealing with remedial service issues is doing trial and error parts replacement, especially when dealing with technology products. The reason being, once a sensitive spare part is unsealed and swapped out, you cannot simply place it back in good inventory. That part must be retested and resealed before it can be reused. Bottom line, honing in on a problem by doing trial and error parts replacement is a very costly practice that should be avoided. The best way to do that, spend more time and money training front-end resources. Meaning, the technicians in the Diagnostics and Dispatch Center, which will undoubtedly prove to be more cost-effective.

9) Maximize customer assisted repairs:

As I have repeatedly stated, the most significant cost item in most CSS organizations is field operations cost. Therefore, anything that can be done to lower field operations cost will positively impact the bottom line. In which case, customer assisted repairs can certainly contribute toward that end.

The biggest challenge service organizations face in this regard is enticing customers to willingly assist in repair activities. Obviously, you must offer customers something in return. In some cases, that may mean a lower contracted service price, which stipulates when and how customer involvement would be required in a repair. In other cases, in which uptime is critical to the client, convince them their participation will get them up and running sooner than waiting for a field technician to arrive at their site. Regardless of the approach taken, both parties (client and vendor) must somehow benefit. Otherwise, expecting customers to assist in repairs due to the *goodness in their hearts* is simply not realistic.

10) Implement an optimal parts logistics strategy:

Parts logistics functions typically include the following three activities: inventory planning, warehousing, and distribution. Furthermore, unlike most other CSS operations functions, which only impact the P&L, parts logistics impacts both the P&L and Balance Sheet. The P&L reflects parts consumption cost, as well as operations management cost for the three above mentioned logistic activities. The P&L is also impacted by excess and obsolete inventory write-offs (more on this in a moment).

The Balance Sheet reflects the value of spare parts inventory, which is principally influenced by two factors. First, ensuring the appropriate amount of inventory is on hand (not materially more or less), which is one of the primary responsibilities of inventory planners. The second, taking necessary and timely actions to deal with excess and obsolete inventory, which means doing periodic reviews to identify unnecessary inventory. If it's determined there is no foreseeable way the quantity of inventory on hand will be consumed, the excess inventory should be written off. Likewise, if you are still carrying spare parts for products that have been deemed obsolete, those parts should also be written off. Simply put, carrying excess and/or obsolete inventory results in overstating assets on your Balance Sheet, as well as under-reporting cost on your P&L, which both represent poor business practices.

Although inventory planning typically represents a relatively small portion of the total logistics budget, how well planners do their job can have a significant impact on both the P&L and Balance Sheet. From a P&L standpoint, ordering optimal part quantities in optimal frequencies matters from an order processing cost standpoint, as does taking advantage of available quantity discounts. On the other hand, doing a sloppy job planning can result in having to write off excess and/or obsolete inventory, which can be very costly. From a Balance Sheet standpoint, having too much inventory on hand could mean tying up capital that could be better used elsewhere in the company. On the other hand, having too little inventory can be equally consequential, particularly from a customer satisfaction standpoint. Imagine how upset a customer would be if you don't have the necessary parts on hand to repair a product on which they are running a business critical application.

There are several viable warehousing and distribution strategies a CSS organization can adopt, including centralized, regional, local, as well as having spare parts in a field technician's van. Some of these strategies can be combined. For example, having a centralized national warehouse, complimented by several regional warehouses, as well as having select common parts in field technicians' vans. On the other hand, a company may simply adopt a single centralized warehousing strategy. In some cases, companies will even rent space in a central distribution company warehouse to stock critical parts that can be immediately distributed, for example, the FEDEX hub in Memphis, TN. The fact of the matter, there is no right or wrong warehousing and distribution strategy. It depends on the size and scope of the CSS organization, as well as the criticality of the businesses they service and support.

11) Implement an optimal repair strategy:

Product Repair Centers are generally responsible for dealing with one or both of the following, repair and return of customer owned whole units and/or repair of defective product components. Whole unit repair and return is a common method of providing warranty support when companies do not offer an exchange option. From a process standpoint, repair and return is slow and inefficient compared to warranty exchange. Incidentally, with regard to exchanges, unless a product fails within the first 30 days of purchase, which many companies consider the DOA period, a defective unit will be replaced with a refurbished unit. Whereas, products that fail during the DOA period are replaced with a new unit.

From a warranty cost standpoint, I would have to say repair and return service is more costly than exchange service. The simple reason, product repairs are handled on an individual basis. Meaning, the very same product the customer sends in for repair is returned to them. On the other hand, the cost of exchange service is lower because returned defective units are typically refurbished in a more cost-efficient production like process. The exchange unit that is sent to the customer is pulled from refurbished inventory, which is a quicker and easier way to get the customer up and running sooner than later. Although most customers prefer an exchange for the stated reason, there are some who prefer repair and return service. The principal reason, they know the level of care their product received. Whereas, an exchange unit may have been neglected and/or overused prior to being refurbished.

Component repair means reconditioning stockpiled defective parts that came about from doing whole unit repairs. From a process standpoint, these components are typically individually repaired on a work bench, as opposed to a production like process. The reason being, each component can have any number of sub-component issues that need to be isolated and rectified.

From a cost standpoint, the most important decision that needs to be made regarding component repair is inventory classification. In other words, should the component be treated as repairable or expendable (throwaway)? Except in unusual short supply situations, the decision usually comes down to cost. In other words, is it more cost-effective to handle and repair defective components versus throwing them away and replacing them with new components? Incidentally, repairable/expendable classifications should periodically be re-evaluated. The reason being, as products evolve toward commoditization, so too components become cheaper. My point being, you do not want to continue fixing components that have become cheaper to buy new.

12) Implement an optimal refurbishment strategy:

Product Return & Refurbishment Centers strictly deal with defective whole units that are either returned for customer credit or swapped for refurbished or new replacement units. As mentioned earlier, products that are deemed defective within 30 days of purchase are generally treated as DOA returns, which means the customer receives a new instead of a refurbished replacement unit. Normally, these centers are centrally located within a nation. For example, in the USA, a company would likely set up a Return & Refurbishment Center in one of the mid-nation Sothern states for both logistical reasons and to take advantage of relatively lower labor cost.

Although these centers are established with good intentions, they sometimes become out of control, and largely turn into scrap centers. Unfortunately, many humans are afflicted with a desire to hold onto *stuff* just in case it is needed in the future. If the managers running these centers possess that *hoarding* mentally, clutter is almost guaranteed to occur. Specifically, I am referring to piles of product caucuses and components that have been stripped from defective returns, which will *never* be used. Those *junk* piles do nothing more than take up valuable space and create unnecessary clutter. The fact of the matter, the cost of tying up warehouse space is probably far greater than the salvage value of those junk piles. That is precisely the reason strictly adhering to documented disposition guidelines and retained only pre-defined maximum levels of both defective and refurbished inventory is the only way to go.

Incidentally, just because defective returns are sent to these centers does not mean they should be refurbished. Refurbishment typically only makes sense for relatively high-cost product. In most cases, companies are better off disposing low-cost defective returns because they are not worth the handling and refurbishing cost. In fact, it may be more cost-effective to simply give the customer a credit, and allow them to keep the defective unit.

13) Cost effectively manage clients:

Once again, over delivering to clients is equally bad for business as is under delivering, from both a revenue and cost standpoint. Generally speaking, over-delivery occurs for the following two reasons. First, consistently delivering above contracted service levels, because your motto is *delighting* customers. Simply put, there is no legitimate business reason for consistently providing a client, let's say, 98% service level when they are contracted to receive 95% performance. It's important to be mindful, delight comes with an extraordinary cost tag. In which case, the underlying question becomes, can you really afford to delight your customers?

The second reason over-delivery occurs is due to customer concessions. Although it's generally considered smart business to *give a little to get a little* (so to speak), consistently allowing customer concessions is unnecessary and costly. For the most part, when customers request extra work that is not covered under the service contract, they should be billed for that work. Otherwise, from a profitability standpoint, there is no way of offsetting the extra cost that will undoubtedly be incurred providing the extra service. The other downside of repeatedly giving away free service, the customer will expect the same to continue for the foreseeable future. If the service provider eventually decides enough is enough, and takes a hard stance regarding future free service, I can almost assure you they will butt heads with spoiled customers, which can lead to other consequences. Therefore, the right thing to do is allow concessions sparingly and selectively. As mentioned earlier, being a little lenient in justifiably reasonable situations can be good for business, while bending over backward is definitely the wrong thing to do.

14) Cost effectively justify human resources:

Simply put, the most cost-effective way of justifying human resources is on the basis of return value. Since service businesses largely consist of people cost, how those people are justified, measured, and managed matters a great deal from a profitability perspective. Unfortunately, many companies do not apply sufficient rigor to their human resource justification process until it's too late. Meaning, at which point they are experiencing financial difficulty, requiring them to tighten their hiring process. Instead of being reactive, businesses need to be more proactive in order to avoid potential downstream consequences. Incidentally, when companies are in reactive mode, the typical management response is launching an across-the-board resource reduction plan and/or severely constrain the resource replacement process.

Generally speaking, most *across- the- board* actions taken by businesses result in undesirable consequences. For example, cutting or holding back on critical customer facing resource replacements is almost guaranteed to have a significant adverse effect on the business and, in particular customer satisfaction.

Since justification of existing resources is rarely practiced in business, I will only reiterate one important point regarding related cost management. Whenever businesses introduce new tools and technology or implement improved business processes, it is essential they also take corresponding resource actions. In other words, if a company has invested in new tools, technology, or process changes, resources that are no longer required as a result of those changes should either be eliminated or assigned elsewhere in the business where they can make worthwhile contributions.

One of the most significant missed resource cost containment opportunities occurs when replacement decisions are being made. The principal reason, most companies treat hiring replacement resources as a foregone conclusion. The flawed logic being, if there was good reason for having the position filled before it was vacated, there is good reason to backfill it now. Instead, management should treat every resource replacement decision as a potential cost reduction opportunity. Meaning, re-evaluate all of the incumbent's activities and eliminate the non-essential ones. If it's reasonably possible, disperse the remaining essential activities amongst existing resources that have available bandwidth. That may mean a broader evaluation of the entire group activities to identify and eliminate additional waste, which can be replaced with the departing employee's critical activities. If those steps do not produce the desired outcome, proceed with the resource replacement hiring.

Moreover, there are situations in which a vacated position can be replaced with a lower job level, which will also result in cost savings. There may be other approaches the hiring manager can consider, such as replacing a vacated position with a new college hire, etc. As Benjamin Franklin famously quoted, *"every problem is an opportunity in disguise"*, which is precisely how each resource replacement decision should be viewed.

With regard to justifying additional resources, one of the major shortcomings is justifying them on the basis of need (or want) rather than return value. Let's face it, investing in additional human resources is essentially no different than investing in additional capital. In which case, capital investments that are not projected to generate a return value greater than the required investment are generally rejected. The same should be true for additional resource justification. In other words, approvals that are based on need (or want) should be far and few. Instead, in most cases, justification should be based on quantifiable return value. If the return value is not greater than the on-going cost of the additional resource, in most cases, those resource requests should be rejected. And yes, there should be some exceptions to that rule. There are times when businesses have to add resources whose return value cannot be quantified, or the cost of that resource will knowingly be greater than the return value. Once again, those exceptions should be *far and few.*

To reiterate what was stated earlier, one factor that will commonly influence the ease or difficulty of getting additional resources approved is the company's current financial condition. When business performance is good, there is typically less rigor applied to the resource hiring process. Meaning, hiring managers have an easier time getting additional resources approved, with or without quantified value justification. Unfortunately, therein lies a problem that must be avoided. Allowing resources to be easily added because the business is doing well is simply not smart. In order to contain unnecessary cost, the same resource justification rigor should be applied, regardless of current business performance. The reason being, shortsighted decisions are almost guaranteed to haunt you later, when business conditions may be more challenging.

15) Maximize direct labor resource utilization:

CSS organizations are clearly labor intensive, in which case direct labor resources make up the lion's share of cost. Therefore, anything that can be done to improve direct resource utilization will definitely improve P&L performance. Along with other tools that can potentially be leveraged to improve direct resource utilization, the following three are among the most impactful: standardization, training and development, and streamlining business processes.

In most service organizations, there is a constant and ever-present challenge to move away from standardized to non-standard processes for individual customers. Everything reasonably possible should be done to resist those challenges. It is an indisputable fact, the more processes are standardized in a service organization, the more cost-effective it will be. Likewise, investing in more training and skill development will typically more than pay for itself by improving direct labor efficiency. And, constantly re-evaluating and streamlining business processes can also have a significant positive impact on direct labor utilization.

Also critical is measuring and managing direct labor utilization as reported in call management and labor tracking systems. Call Management Systems report measurements such as: number of calls taken and resolved, average call duration, and more. The reported measurements can help managers hone in on specific areas call center agents need to improve individual performance. Utilization reports generated from Field Service Management Systems can do likewise for field technicians. In a typical CSS organization, the reporting that is generated from the two above mentioned systems cover a large portion of the total direct labor population. In most cases,

I would say well over 80% of the direct labor force is tied to one of those two systems. Therefore, analyzing and acting on reported utilization data can potentially go a long way toward improving profitability.

16) Minimize use of marginal value indirect labor resources:

With the exception of small mom and pop operations, indirect labor resources, which can be broadly categorized as overhead, are essential in most businesses. It's hard to imagine running a viable business without Management, Finance, Human Resources, and Legal. Therefore, the question regarding overhead resources is not whether or not they are needed. Instead, the question should be, how many are necessary and justifiable on the basis of cost versus return value? Unfortunately, most companies do not approach indirect resource hiring decisions with payback value in mind, which is the principal reason many companies end up with more indirect resources than can be economically justified.

Indirect resources normally fall into two categories. They are either project oriented or part of general overhead, such as Finance, Legal, etc. Generally speaking, I'd say project oriented resources typically prove more worthwhile than resources that are permanently added to an organization. The principal reason, project resources are usually assigned to time-defined projects, which size and scope are clearly defined beforehand. Furthermore, the cost versus return value of project resources can be objectively evaluated before undertaking a project. The same cannot be said for permanent indirect resources, which are oftentimes not value justifiable. As a matter of fact, those resources tend to continually creep up in organizations for the following two predominant reasons.

First, growth in indirect resources is often linear with growth in business, which is simply not prudent in most businesses. With growth, businesses will almost certainly have to add some indirect resources. However, along with growth should come more efficiency, not more waste.

The second predominant reason for indirect resource creep is classic management overreaction to problems or issues that have arisen in the business. Meaning, they oftentimes add permanent financial or business analysts to address the new challenges. Generally speaking, those are precisely the type of resources that are needed to analyze and help resolve business problems and issues. But, why do those resources have to be permanently added to the organization? Wouldn't it make more sense to bring in temporary resources for what is often a one-time problem or issue? I've seen this classic management overreaction occur time and again, particularly as it applies to financial analysts and business analysts. Bottom line, it simply makes no sense to add permanent resource cost to a business when temporary resources would be more cost-effective.

By the way, there is always a so-called *good reason* to add another indirect resource to an organization to do more counting, control, and/or analyze business activity. The fact of the matter, this behavior will often contribute to lopsided situations in which indirect labor cost represents an ever-growing percentage of total labor cost. Don't allow that to happen in your business. Remember, regardless of whether cost is spent wisely or frivolously, it has the same impact on the business bottom line. In which case, the more cost can be avoided, the better will be the P&L results.

17) Effectively manage and control resource vendor cost:

CSS organizations often utilize external resources to either augment internal field service capabilities or in lieu of internal resources. A fundamental question that should always be asked when contemplating resource decisions, is it better to use internal or external resources? For the most part, decisions whether or not to go with external resources comes down to two primary considerations, economics and risk.

With regard to the economic aspect, you must carefully consider all related internal and external cost factors in order to produce a true *apple to apples* comparison. For example, external resource cost is not simply a measurement of what you pay the resource vendor. To that base cost, you must add client management oversight, training, and attrition cost. Likewise, employee gross salary does not represent total internal cost. To that base cost, you must add fringe and other employee related overhead, which typically adds up to approximately 50% of gross salary.

With regard to risk, it comes to one major factor. Will the external resources provide your customers with the same quality level service and support as internal resources? Incidentally, managing risk generally represents a balancing act between rewards (cost savings) and consequences (adverse customer impact).

Taking advantage of low-cost offshore resources is enticing, especially for companies or organizations that are attempting to either preserve or improve profitability. However, it is also important to be aware there are inherent risks associated with offshoring. Meaning, it will not always prove to be the best or most cost-effective choice. At first glance, offshoring will almost always be appealing because it provides access to low-cost resources. However, unless there is considerable effort and care applied to the planning, design, and rollout of the offshore solution, the cost advantage can quickly dissipate. Incidentally, CSS organizations are likely to utilize offshore resources for call center support (both technical and customer services), and to a lesser extent for some back office operations, such as order and billing administration. The reason for those limitations, much of CSS service and support is provided locally at customer sites.

The attitude and willingness to utilize low-cost offshore resources has changed over the past several years, principally as a result of competitive cost pressures. More and more companies are forced to look externally for low-cost resource solutions just to remain competitive. In the final analysis, decisions regarding resources come down to where the work can be done cheaper, better, faster, while maximizing profitability. That said, it's important to be mindful, most organizations will face challenges implementing a successful offshore solution. Two of the most common challenges include quality control and resource retention. The primary reason for the latter, other companies often compete for the same precious offshore resources. In which case, companies that are willing to pay highest wages will usually attract the largest share of available resources. By the way, when resources move around for higher wages, which is very common in parts of the world low-cost resources are available, it creates incremental training and attrition cost challenges for companies that are losing those resources.

Finally, I'd like to add, from a best practices standpoint, resource vendors must be held accountable for the same end-client deliverables the CSS organization is accountable. That way, both parties share responsibility for providing end-client contracted deliverables. Vendor agreements that do not mention or loosely define end-client deliverables can be detrimental to CSS. Meaning, any and all non-performance consequences will rest totally with CSS instead of being shared with the vendor. For both customer satisfaction and profitability reasons, holding vendors accountable for their delivery performance is essential.

Managing Revenue Business Drivers

Below is a list of notable CSS revenue drivers, which will be followed by a detailed explanation of each item:

1. Bill clients for delivered service level and minimize concessions.

2. Aggressively market and sell extended warranty and post-warranty service contracts.

3. Maximize time and material (T&M) billing.

4. Consider selling service contracts to support co-located other vendor products.

1) Bill clients for delivered service level and minimize concessions:

Ad previously mentioned in the *cost drivers* section, delivering materially higher or lower than contracted service level is equally bad for business, from both a revenue and cost perspective.

There are two distinct ways over-delivery generally occurs. The first, the service provider consistently delivers above contracted service levels. In other words, if the contracted service level is to achieve 95% repair incident resolution within eight hours, consistently achieving 98% represents over-delivery. Although over-delivery may be viewed favorably by the client, it's clearly an unnecessary cost and potentially a lost revenue opportunity for CSS. In other words, if the client truly wants or needs 98% performance, they should pay for the higher service level.

The other way over-delivery occurs is when customer concessions are allowed. In other words, not billing for the extra work the client has requested. It's okay to allow clients occasional concessions. As a matter of fact, I personally believe it's good business, but only to a limit. Even though concession is generally a dirty word in business, it's oftentimes viewed as a cost of doing business. That is particularly true for long-standing and/or strategic clients, which a reasonable amount of cooperative give and take will almost always result in a better client/vendor relationship.

On the other hand, if you allow your client to push you around, demanding more and more concessions for the privilege of doing business with them, you have lost control. And, more importantly, you probably also lose the client's respect.

If you haven't experienced this first hand, allow me to explain how concessions play a role in normal and healthy business to business relationships. Once a lengthy and detailed service contract is signed, most customers want to be able to place that document on the shelf and refer to it only when it is absolutely necessary. If the delivery or client manager is constantly waving the service contract in front of the client, pointing out what's included and excluded from the agreement, the client will surely become increasingly frustrated. Consequently, instead of gaining an ally and potentially a good reference account, which is valued like gold in business, you will almost certainly create an adversarial relationship with your client.

By the way, no reasonable client is going to expect most everything they request over and above contracted deliverables to be done for free. As usual, the best solution is finding that sensible middle ground where both parties give a little to get a little in return. Bottom line, aside from potentially allowing a few customer satisfaction concessions, the delivery or client manager must make sure the client is billed for the services that are delivered. The best way to ensure that is done is to present the client with a Charge Order whenever they request relatively significant out-of-scope services. Let the small stuff go, which most customers will appreciate and will likely pay dividends in the future, in terms of expanded and/or new business opportunities.

2) Aggressively market and sell extended warranty and post-warranty service contracts:

As stated earlier, extended warranty and post-warranty service contracts can be lucrative on the condition that quality, reliability, and serviceability is built into the products. On the other hand, if companies introduce products into the marketplace that clearly do not possess those attributes, I can almost guarantee the cost to support service contracts will most likely exceed the corresponding revenue.

With regard to selling service contracts, there are essentially three different ways it can be done. The first and most cost-effective method is selling them at product point of sale. The reason being, there is virtually no selling cost involved. In fact, it's typically just a matter of adding a line item to the product invoice or bill of sale. This method is most commonly used for relatively low-priced products sold by retailers and resellers. The second, and generally least cost-effective selling method, is utilizing a dedicated sales team within the CSS organization. Such a team would only be cost justifiable if the size of the CSS business unit is significant. The third, and most common selling method used for relatively higher priced product, is leveraging the company's general sales force. However, getting the sales force attention may be challenging. The reason being, incentives for service contract sales are generally significantly lower than incentives for relatively higher priced product sales.

There are a couple different ways of getting salespeople attention. One, offer a higher percentage sales incentive for service contracts than product sales. The other, mandate a certain percentage of product sales be accompanied by a service contract, in order for salespeople to maximize their incentive compensation.

3) Maximize time and material (T&M) billing:

Unlike profit generated from service contracts, which depends on the amount of service cost incurred supporting those contracts, T&M profit is generally high for one primary reason. Customers are typically billed for labor and parts at list price. However, the down side of T&M business, it is not consistent. Furthermore, when T&M billing volume is high, the service provider will often be confronted with the following consequential challenge. Customers who have to pay for T&M service will often point to product lacking quality and reliability, which may very well affect customer attitudes toward future purchases.

4) Consider selling service contracts to support co-located other vendor products:

Service infrastructure typically represents a substantial investment. Therefore, service organizations often look for ways to help recover that investment. One way is to offer service contracts for co-located other vendor products. Although that may be beneficial for the service organization, in terms of additional business, it can be challenging acquiring other vendor proprietary repair parts at reasonable prices. For the client, it could represent a win on two counts: less multi-vendor finger pointing when service issues arise, and a high probability of obtaining a more competitive service contract price. For the service organization, it is an additional way of defraying some infrastructure cost, as well as represent an additional revenue and profit opportunity.

Closing Comments

Regardless of the reason you picked up and decided to read this book, I hope you found it beneficial in some way or another. For those of you who are involved in a service business (whether it's CSS or other service business), your own experiences can now be coupled with the experiences I have shared. Without question, learning from one's own experience is always best. Second best is learning from someone else's shared experience, which was precisely my intent writing this book.

For those of you who are not involved in a service business, but maybe aspire to do so in the future, this book may serve as a good *jump start*. And, for those of you who were simply drawn to the book because the title caught your eye, welcome to the world of services. In any case, it's personally gratifying to know that I have shared information and real-life experiences that may somehow be useful and helpful to others.

Finally, I would like make the following comments. Taking advantage of the many profit improvement ideas I shared is a good thing. On the other hand, taking advantage of your clients is *not*. Just as I have preached the importance of return value throughout the book, customers expect the same for money they spend on services. Once they sense their service provider has taken advantage of them, you can say goodbye to those customers. Getting them back or finding replacement customers is almost guaranteed to be more costly than the incremental profit you may have generated from greedy practices. Be fair and respectful to all of your customers, and they will be loyal in return. In service businesses, customer loyalty is one of the most important keys to success.

www.ingramcontent.com/pod-product-compliance
Lightning Source LLC
Chambersburg PA
CBHW051456170526
45166CB00001B/263